WRITE YOUR OWN PAYCHECK

8 Simple Steps To Financial Independence

Katharina Thiessen, B.Ed.
Licensed Financial Services Rep., Investor

Aunt Sara, you have a very special place in my heart, thanks for always taking time for me when I am in your neighbourhood!

Much love:

Kathy

Nov. 2019

Write Your Own Paycheck- 8 Simple Steps to Financial Independence.
www.YourOwnPayToday.com
Copyright © 2019 Katharina Thiessen
ISBN: 978-1-77277-316-3

Publisher
10-10-10 Publishing
Markham, ON Canada

Printed in Canada and the United States of America

Table of Contents

I dedicate this book to my beautiful children,
Eberhard, Carl, and Rachel,
and my lovely grandson, Nathaniel.
You are my reason to win,
my motivation and my pride.
I love you so much.

Foreword

If financial statements or concepts seem boring to you, *Write Your Own Paycheck* is a book that will grab your attention. Author Katharina Thiessen writes in clear and simple ways, with explanations about financial matters that will inspire you. Not only will you be able to understand how to build your financial plan, but you will also learn how to reach your desired retirement goal, from where you are right now.

No matter your age, or stage in life, Katharina writes and teaches on every aspect of a solid financial plan.

Write Your Own Paycheck is not just about understanding how money works. It's about your habits and your attitude. It's about planning and embracing changes.

Knowing less can cost you more. After you read *Write Your Own Paycheck*, you will have the knowledge and understanding of how to make money work for you.

Embrace changes and expect to succeed. If you will apply what Katharina teaches in this book, rest assured you will have peace of mind.

Raymond Aaron
New York Times Bestselling Author

Acknowledgements

I dedicate this book to my dear children, **Eberhard, Carl,** and **Rachel**, and my sweet grandson, **Nathaniel**, who shows his love for books by sneaking to bed at night with a book under his blanket.

To my dear parents, J**ohn and Tina Thiessen,** who taught me great work ethics and persistency.

To my **Grandma and Grandpa Thiessen,** who are gone now but were huge campaigners for literature, and shared their books with me.

I dedicate this book to my dear ex-mother-in-law, **Susana:** You have made such a tremendous impact in my life with your caring love for all your children, and you taught me all your special skills. You are a true pearl, beautiful inside and out. I love you.

To my dear sister, **Susan**, and family, who always received me with open arms, and house, during my visits to B.C.

To my dear sister, **Lisa,** who has that special touch to lift people up with a good spirit. You are the born counsellor.

To all my other siblings, who have their unique spot in my life.

To my violin teacher, **Iliana Fileva**, who was not only my teacher but also a mother and dear friend to me in the darkest time in my life.

To my dear God-sent friend, **Julian**, your sense of humour and encouragement was always there. "Never give up on your dreams, and always look for better ways," was highlighted in our conversations. I am so blessed to have you in my friend circle, and I have learned so much from you—even English when I was new to Canada. Muchas gracias querido amigo!

To my beautiful friend, **Selene Castillo,** who always saw the good in people, and motivated me to do the same. With your beautiful voice, you enrich peoples lives. You are beautiful inside and out. Te amo amiga!

To my lovely friend, **Maria Penner de Reimer,** we had so many good hours and conversations together. Volleyball evenings definitely were a big part of our friendship. Te extraño y te quiero mucho.

To **Ron and Carol Neusteter,** and **John and Ruth Janzen,** you are true friends, and you have a special place in my heart.

Heidi Wall, Eva Penner, Eva Pando, Crisol Gonzalez, Jonie Rempel, Nathalie Dyck, Gil Ruiz, Mary Fehr, Maria and Lucy Rempel, Rosa Heide, Lily Fehr, Martha Penner, and Maria Dyck: You are very special to me, and our love for music has knit us together.

To my numerous students at school and at private music lessons, through you I was blessed, and I thank all of you. There are too many of you to write your individual names.

To **Pastor John, Sharon**, and my care group in Manitoba, and the whole church family, you are so dear to me.

To the staff at Salem Home, I had great joy working together with you; you are continuing the wonderful service. To **Katherine Peters** and the staff at Comforts of Home Care, I was blessed to work with you.

A big thank you to my dear aunt **Sara**, your kindred spirit is priceless and my highlights in B.C. are the moments you and I spend together.

Thank you to **Gladys Thiessen**, you are beautiful inside and out. I love you!

Lisa Suderman, Elena Rempel and Anne Thiessen, you know how special you are, and that you are a blessing to me. You are real troopers.

To **Henry and Susie Dyck, Esther Omoleye, Tina Fast, Aida and Odie, Tina Rempel**, and the rest of my team in British Columbia, Alberta, Manitoba, and Ontario; to **Evan Giesbrecht, Steve Elias, Helen and Carolina, Peter**, and all the other colleagues in Winkler, Winnipeg, and North York—it is a real joy to have you all in my life as dear friends.

A special thank you goes to my wonderful CEO, **Colleen Trautman**, who is always there to support, teach, and lead by example.

A big thank you to **JP and Catherine Labossiere**, and **Tina and Willy Siemens**, for your ongoing mentorship.

My accountability partners, **Steven and Reneta,** you were making sure that I got this book done and out.

A very special thank you to my Mastermind Alliance Group; you are always there for me and cheer me on. Our morning reading hours have been a true blessing; we have bonded, and brainstorming with you guys was definitely a highlight of each day. When you asked how the book was coming, you didn't want to hear about the labour pains; you just wanted to see the baby. Here you have it.

I know I have missed many, many, many names, but I want you to know, if you know me, you have been a blessing in my life.

And of course, I dedicate this book to my dear friend, **Aslan**; you are a true inspiration! With your caring and loving attitude, and the knowledge and wisdom you possess, you have been a true blessing to me. Thanks for the many great tips you shared with me. You are priceless!

Praise for *Write Your Own Paycheck*

Not so long ago, after a Paradigm Shift seminar with Bob Proctor, Katharina told me that she got inspired to write a book; and today, I am holding this manuscript in my hands. She followed her dreams!

Katharina has grown so much as a person! I have watched this girl go from having a full-time job to starting her own business and writing her own paycheck.

As I read this book, I see a clear roadmap to financial independence, outlined in a simple way that anyone can learn. You will be taken on a journey, with simple steps that you can learn and apply to accomplish your dreams in life.

- Tina Siemens, Senior Marketing Director with World Financial Group; instructor of the Financial Education Foundation Program in Lethbridge, Alberta; Insurance Agent; MF Rep. Financial Literacy Campaigner.

I met Katharina for the first time at a trade show in Cuauhtémoc Chihuahua, Mexico, and I saw a true entrepreneur in her.

At first, I thought she was a "Gringa" (that's what we Mexicans call the white people), but she told me that she is German but was born in Mexico. I wanted to learn more about her and her culture. Something intrigued me about her, and I soon learned that she was not only an entrepreneur but also a music teacher and a member of a string orchestra. She invited me to her upcoming concert, and we have kept in touch ever since, even though she has moved to Canada.

Katharina is a true inspiration to everyone who wants to be successful. With her positive attitude and belief in people, she will always go the extra mile; and in this book, she points out how you can change your life by changing the way you think. Finances play a big role in our lives, but if we don't have a winning mindset—which she points out throughout this book—little will change.

Katharina is always ready to learn new things and help other people.

She believes in STOP LEARNING...STOP EARNING!!

She inspires me to be a successful and better person! I wish her a lot of success in everything she undertakes.

- *Julian Renteria Marin, Bachelor Degree in Commercial Relations, Technological Institute of Chihuahua; Real Estate Agent; Entrepreneur.*

"Be the light in the darkness,
A guide at night.
Hope for the weary,
Be the light,
Shine,
Be the light."

– Katharina Thiessen

∞ Chapter One ∞

Dare to Dream

*"Cherish your vision and your dreams as
they are the children of your soul,
the blueprints of your ultimate achievements."*
- Napoleon Hill

The Child in You

No matter what age you are today or where you find yourself—no matter if you are just starting your own financial plan or if you are a middle-aged person or retired already—we all can think back to when we were a child, and I'm asking you to do just that right now.

I remember as though it were yesterday, when my younger sister was born, and she had to have surgery on a hernia. I watched my Aunt Betty take care of the wound and, at that moment, I knew that one day I wanted to care for sick people. I was 2 and 1/2 years old at that time. I cannot remember if I was able to speak at that age. I probably was, but what I remember is the thought that I wanted to care for sick people, and it always stayed with me.

About five years later, when my youngest sister was born, I was going to school already, and my dreams now expanded to not only the huge dream I had when I was two, but to also wanting to be a teacher. School, books, and particularly numbers fascinated me ever since I started kindergarten, and this continued all throughout school. But I remember that after school, my two sisters would make plans to play with their dolls; and me, being a very hyperactive child, was not too fond of playing along with them. I would rather make the suggestion that if their dolls had any health issues, I could treat them with medicine, and they could be sure about having "healthy kids" soon after. Now, that didn't happen too many times. But when it happened, I was born ready to give them a needle or do surgery or some sort of treatment. My poor little sisters did not like to see their "kids" going through all those medical procedures with this *wannabe* doctor, and decided that their dolls wouldn't get sick anymore.

As an eight or nine-year-old "doctor," I was out of business now, but I did not let that affect me a single bit. I called on my imaginary people, declared many of them to be sick, and was back in business again. That worked better anyway, as no one disagreed with me, and the turnout was always to everyone's liking. You get my point.

But I also changed my "career," and I now had way more success being a teacher for my sisters than a doctor for their "kids."

When you were a child, what dreams did you have? We see kids playing with so much enthusiasm and imagination that no matter how many times an older sibling or a parent reminds them that it's all just imagination and not real, they won't stop dreaming. But then, one day, the kid gets tired of hearing over and over again that what seems so real to them is not real, and they start to suppress their dreams, feelings, and imaginings.

I want you to take a moment here and think back to when you were a child. What dreams or imaginings did you have? Have those dreams become reality for you now? Or have they been nicely tucked away, all but forgotten? Let's go into that drawer or filing cabinet of your brain and take away all those layers that block your dreams from coming to the surface, and start dreaming again.

As kids, we have no limitations of what we can do. In our imaginations, everything is possible. Our minds are wide open, and we only shrink our dreams by following adult advice to get real, stop dreaming, and use common sense. Does that sound familiar to you? Instead of being encouraged to explore our imaginations, walls are created that keep us in bondage. Let's take a look at when we get older...

The Teenager in You

As a teenager, we are generally risk-takers, aren't we?

Can you remember situations, circumstances, or scenarios where you took a huge risk as a teenager—where you would ask yourself: What would my parents have said if they had known?

Why did we take risk in the first place? Was it because of curiosity, or the excitement of the journey? And again, with a lot of imagination mixed into it?

I was a Tomboy as a teenager, and I loved to hang out with my older brother, who was over two years older than me and many centimeters taller. I would climb the same trees and the same mountains he did, and often with his help. We took the risk of falling down, which somehow didn't happen too often. We held onto branches that barely would hold our weight, at heights of 40 feet. We would stand on cliffs that were hundreds of feet high, just to have the thrill of looking down at the people in the valley, and waving at them to show off how high up we had made it. We were risk-takers by nature.

I remember that my brother and I would often hide our activities from our parents or older siblings. We couldn't talk freely about our adventures and the risk we exposed ourselves to. I can imagine, now that I am older, that it would've been a huge benefit to us if our parents had taken the time to talk to us about our risk-taking, and not just tell us not to try and explore as we liked to. I am not blaming my parents for what they did or did not do; they did their best with what they knew at that time.

What is your story? Were you a risk-taker in your teens? Are you still a risk- taker? Next, let's take a look at the adult...

The Adult in You

Are you still the dreamer, with all kinds of imagination, or the risk-taker that you possibly were in your teens?

Over the years, in my adulthood, I have observed thousands of people who have very little imagination left, who stopped dreaming and who walk through life like noheads.

I asked myself why that is. Is that because someone, when we were young, told us to stop dreaming? Is it because we were taught by our parents, teachers, or even our church to fit in and act like everyone else, and to do the same things the generation did before us, or is it because our society has a huge impact on what we do, say, and think?

When I train my team, I find that I work with smart people. It's not that they aren't able to learn new skills, but they have to get rid of their beliefs that they can't do it. This not only limits us in making the kind of money we want or applying for a job that we like; it limits us in all aspects of our lives. I encourage you, if you would like to do things that you feel are too big for you or appear impossible, to dare to dream again. Use your imagination. If you can see it in your mind, you can hold it in your hands.

People who lack vision, perish. We are all meant to create, expand, and seek growth to be successful.

I'm teaching an online seminar on "The Art of Goal Creation," where I show a set of ideas to help you dream, plan, visualize, and take action, to not only set goals but to also understand the psychology behind it, to literally help you see the process unfolding. If you would like access to the seminar, go to my website, www.YourOwnPayToday.com, for more information.

The Senior in You

Julia had moved into a seniors' home. She was a happy lady and always had stuff going on to pass the time. When the aids came to check on her, she would ask them to look at her crafts or the pictures on the wall, and she would share about her family. Her boys were now grown up and running their own businesses, and her girls had their own busy lives. She would also tell them so many things about her grandchildren that she adored. For Julia, there was no dull moment. Had dementia not taken over, she would still be at home, but she needed someone to care for her because her mind didn't give her clear direction at all times, and her family couldn't be with her during their working times. The aids were lucky to have her, as she was such a cheerful resident. However, life hadn't always been easy for her. She had lost her first husband and had gone through some very tough years. She married a second time, and lost her second husband in her late 70s; but she had kept a positive mindset and kept her spirits up. One thing that people admired about her was her spirit; she wouldn't give up on dreaming of new projects for the next day, like crafting a gift for one of her grandchildren's birthdays.

When we hit our senior years, we can't go back and live our lives again, or do things that we regret not having done. We can do things today that will make a difference tomorrow in our own lives or in someone else's life.

Be the person today that you will be proud of tomorrow. Look into the future with a positive mindset.

∞ Bonus: Goal Creation Tips – See:
www.YourOwnPayToday.com

∞ Questions for Success ∞

* What is the most helpful idea from this chapter for you?

* Which age group are you in from those four mentioned in this chapter?

* Which age group do you identify with the most?

* What is your biggest dream in life?

*Below, write the dreams that you want to accomplish in your life:

1._____

_____

2._____

_____

Write Your Own Paycheck

3._____

_____

4._____

_____

*"You have within you, right now,
everything you need to deal
with whatever the world
can throw at you."*
- Brian Tracy

∞ Chapter Two ∞

HABITS, Step 1

"Keep your thoughts positive
Because your thoughts become
YOUR WORDS.

Keep your words positive
Because your words become
YOUR BEHAVIOUR.

Keep your behaviour positive
Because your behaviour becomes
YOUR HABITS.

Keep your habits positive
Because your habits become
YOUR VALUES.

Keep your values positive
Because your values become
YOUR DESTINY!"

– Mahatma Gandhi

Your Savings Habits

Have you heard the saying, *how you do anything is how you do everything*?

When I first heard that, I thought to myself that it can't be true. I can do one thing very well but lack resilience in another. But the phrase stuck with me, and I started to reflect on it; and I soon realized that there was truth to it. I think you will agree when you think of the to-do list that you made for the day, promising yourself to get it all done, but then the day starts messing up your schedule, and now you are not only falling short on completing it, but you are off-focus on the next item on your list.

Here's another example: You're determined to stay on budget. Last month, you were off; but this month, you will write everything down that you spend your money on, and not go over budget. But wait, you forgot that your niece's birthday is on Thursday, and you always buy her a gift... You sigh and say that you will save more next month, and then you go and get the gift.

Another example: You are scheduled to meet your child's teacher at school, and you don't want to be late because you respect other people's time. You have to make a short phone call that you almost forgot about because you were so busy, but the call goes on longer than you had expected, and now you have to rush, and you somehow misplaced your keys, and you spend another few minutes to finally find them. Once on the road, almost every streetlight is red, and you get to your appointment 5 minutes late. You feel horrible about it, but it won't happen again!

You get my point? I don't have to continue with more examples, do I?

Now, let's look at our habits, and really make a good habit that you can follow. A habit doesn't get formed overnight; it needs repetition over a long period of time, and it works best when you are accountable to someone. It is only successful when you stay true to yourself!

How you do anything is how you do everything!

Have you ever been in line at a grocery store, and every cash register has a lineup, but the one you're in has this lady ahead of you with a whole stack of coupons, and you watch her checking every single item in the flyer, comparing her coupons with the items she is buying? She argues with the clerk about why she isn't allowed to take 3 items at the discounted price, instead of only two.

You have things to do, and the couple behind you are trying to calm down their three-year-old and are anxious to pay for their groceries and get out of the store.
The lady in front of you has a saving habit when it comes to making every penny count.

When you hear someone saying that they can save $5 on an item if they buy it at a different store that is all the way across town from their place (they always buy that specific item there, but they like to buy the rest at the supermarket), are they saving money?

While you are shopping, you see a few items for half the regular price, but you just bought these items last week and have enough left for at least a month—should you buy now while it's half price?

You go online on Amazon and see shoes for only a few bucks. You have your shoe rack full of shoes, and your subconscious mind tells you that you don't need any new shoes, but you think that the price is so low (just $10) that you will barely notice the difference in your bank account, and you go ahead and check out—but oh no, you still need to pay for shipping! Well, too late, your emotions are already involved with wearing those shoes, so you just go ahead and pull your credit card out, and you type in the numbers and finish your order. Did you save money?

You can answer these questions for yourself, but let me ask you this: Have you ever used one of these methods for saving?

I could go into many more scenarios, like having mortgage insurance vs personal insurance, or term vs whole life or even universal life. Is a cheaper premium always cheaper in the long run?

What about buying a car with cash vs a car loan or lease?

These are all topics to discuss with clients when they meet with me for a financial makeover.

Finances can be tricky, and one size fits all can't be applied here. We don't learn about finances in school. If we did, it's because our teacher went the extra mile to share his or her knowledge with us, outside the school curriculum. But there is way more to personal finances, and it all depends on the individual and his or her circumstances, to build a financial plan that will get them safely through life and beyond. Why is it that a lot of people feel more comfortable talking to their neighbour, mechanic, brother-in-law, or friend about money, than with a financial professional? Is it because, most of the time, they all have the same amount of earnings, and the same amount of savings, and most the time, they all spend the money before they even get paid? We need a financial coach who is licensed and can teach us the difference between the options we have, and who can also structure a plan that creates the results we need in order to have financial security— someone who can teach us discipline and focus, and helps us to stay on track.

Many people understand savings as putting money into a GIC or having it in a savings account at the bank. That may be a good choice for someone who wants to accumulate some money and not have it at home where it is too accessible to spend, but you have to ask yourself: Is the money safe that way? If it's losing buying power, you should not have it in those accounts.

A client of mine loves to buy gifts for his kids and his grandkids, which he does on Black Friday or Boxing Day. When he told me all about it, I soon realized that he actually bought way more gifts than he first intended, because of the discounts he got. He now spent the same amount of money as he would have at regular price. Yes, he got more products for his buck, but did he actually save money?

I could go on and on about our *savings habits* that may seem like saving but usually are not.

The state of your savings does have a lot to do with how tall you walk. Your savings affect the way you stand, the way you walk, the tone of your voice, your physical well-being, and your self-confidence.

A person with savings can walk tall. He or she may appraise opportunities in a relaxed way, have time for judicious estimates, and not be rushed by economic necessity.

A person with savings can afford the wonderful privilege of being generous in family and neighbourhood emergencies.

The ability to save has nothing to do with the size of your income. Many high-income people spend it all, and many low-income people have savings set aside.

Your Spending Habits

When I come to my office in Toronto in the morning, I see many people carrying a cup of coffee that they picked up at their favourite coffee shop. Now, that may be okay, but if people get grumpy because they didn't get their coffee, then that is more than just randomly picking up a coffee—there's a habit involved already. What about brewing your own coffee at home and taking it with you in a travel mug? Maybe pick up a coffee once in a while—but every day, or even a few times a day? Many people don't think about how much money they spend on Tim's or Starbucks, until they put numbers on paper, and then they are shocked at what that same amount of money could do for them if they invested it in an 8% compounding investment over 20 years.

If you're working for wages or salary, you may hear some of your co-workers telling you what they bought on their credit card, and that they can't wait to get their pay so that they can pay off the balance; or they already have it all planned out what the money from their next pay check will go towards. We talk about spending all the time, but what about saving for the unexpected or for our golden years? Do we give that enough thought?

When we look at today's stats, it tells us that 46% of Canadians are only $200 away from financial insolvency, but we have only a low rate of unemployment. Where lies the problem? Many people even have two or three jobs. What are the stats in the USA or in other countries?

I hope the previous paragraph will raise awareness, if nothing else, to really stop and think for a moment where we as North Americans are heading!

Social media doesn't do us much good when we see #fomo, #ootd, etc., and all the selfies showing off.

Can you still be disciplined? Many even buy gifts for people they don't like, with money they don't have. Stop caring so much for people who probably don't even think of you at all. It's none of your business what people think of you, but it's up to you to be smart with your money.

You may say, "I didn't learn about money in school," or, "I don't understand how money works; what is the best thing to do?" That is why you have this book—to give you a big deal of insight on money matters. It's not a get-rich-quick scheme that you will learn in the next pages, but I can tell you that if you apply what you learn here, you will become financially independent over time.

In Canada, we have the Dollar Stores, and our friends south of the border have the Dollaramas, where we can find items for cheap. We have to be mindful though that we don't fool ourselves into thinking that buying cheap saves us money. Nothing against those stores—I go there for some low-priced items sometimes too—but I have found myself buying a pen that was completely dried out, and my $1 cheap pen wasted $1. If we could only learn from our mistakes or other people's, we would do many things different, wouldn't we? Remember, buying cheap items usually costs more. Just a thought...

> *"Take waste out of your spending,*
> *and you'll drive the haste out of your life."*
> – J.P. Morgan

How Organized Are You?

You may wonder what being organized has to do with money matters. My answer here: How you do anything is how you do everything.

I devote this chapter to anyone who wants to be well-organized—me included.

While I'm writing these words, I can think of many areas in my house where I could do a much better job at being organized (for example, my closet, drawers, or office). I find myself putting things down somewhere "for now," as I will "put them in the designated place in just a minute;" but then anything could come up in the next little while that would require my attention, and before I know it, my keys are missing, or my jacket hangs over the chair instead of in the closet—and where is my handbag? Oh yeah, it'll be on the couch or in the kitchen, or you name it, as I did not pay attention to where I put it because I was taking a call as I was going into the house. Does this sound like you? This is especially true for women, who have a spaghetti-woven brain and are always multitasking. But it doesn't have to be like that. I raised two boys, and shared offices and board rooms with male colleagues long enough to know (most of the time, they ask for an item before they start looking for it themselves) that overall, men may be more organized than women.

The reason why being organized is so important is because it saves us a lot of time that we otherwise spend on looking for things. It is also our job to have things put away in an orderly way so that we can quickly find what we're looking for—like our insurance policies, statements, tax filings, receipts, bills, etc.

I once visited one of my clients in her home; we were looking into setting up an RESP for her two little boys. She walked to her bookshelf, pulled out a thick binder, came back to the table, and opened the binder, which was labelled perfectly in alphabetical order and had absolutely all their financial affairs in it. In a few minutes, we had a clear picture of what needed to be done to open the plan, and how much they were able to contribute to the plan. I spent only a very short time with her before we had their plan all set up, and it saved her and me a lot of time.

You may have a different way of organizing your financial documents, and that is perfectly fine. The thing is to have a method that works well for you, and to get it done that way all the time. Then it will save you not just time but also a lot of money.

If you get your bills in the mail, being organized will help you to not have them end up in the recycle bin. If you pay your bills online, set up automatic payments, which will prevent late payments and extra bank charges.

Be organized, and have peace of mind.

The Procrastinator in You

Human beings are procrastinators by nature. Some just have learned more control over it than others.

An acquaintance of mine confessed to me one day that he would notice that the fuel level was very low when he came home from work in the evening, but he made the same old decision, time and time again, to fill up in the morning on his way to work. And then he would end up being late leaving the house in the morning, with not enough time to go to the filling station before going to work. Because of putting it off in the evening, he now not only had to do it in the morning, but he also was late for work. This is just one example, and you may have already said, "Yes, that's me!"

When I worked in healthcare, some years ago, I had to wear scrubs; and a few of them needed ironing—guess what? Before I had to leave for work, they were still all wrinkled, sitting right on the ironing board. Do you think that I had to rush to get them to look decent? Yes! Let me ask you, can you recall an episode where your laundry garments weren't ready when you needed them? Don't answer. Just make the committed decision to stop procrastinating all together.

I have to admit that I am an introvert—I mean for real. My very best friends are my four walls, and I do like to spend a lot of time with them, not that they care at all—but you know, I am a very faithful friend. If I could do all my grocery shopping online, and have them delivered to my door, I wouldn't mind at all. I find because I dread going out, this makes me procrastinate in many cases. But how does this relate now to an extrovert? They have no problem being among people, and although I can't tell from personal experience, I do believe, because of being out and about, things can get pushed off to the next day.

Again, I will mention here, how you do anything is how you do everything; and I encourage you, and myself, to not leave for the next day what you can do today.

Tips for Creating Good Habits

I do believe that most people have good intentions to do better, and we don't plan to fail, but we fail to plan. Don't you think so? A few years ago, I was on my way to Sun Peaks, British Columbia, leaving from Winnipeg, Manitoba. I had a connecting flight, which gave me some time at the airport to look through the bookstore close to my gate. I found this cute little book, called a productivity planner, and it caught my attention. I bought the planner, and I use it as a tool to help me plan my day using the Pomodoro technique of 25 minutes at a time, planning what is the most important task for me to do the following day, and how much time I will need for the specific task. This really has helped me to stay on track and focus, as I set my timer before I start my task, and I don't check my phone or do any other thing during those 25 minutes. Then I give myself five minutes for a break, and then I go right to the next Pomodoro of 25 minutes, to complete the task or just continue working on it. Some tasks take me a few days, and others take only 20 minutes; but regardless, it has been very helpful to have and use the planner. The planner now goes with me everywhere.

You know, our habits have much to say about how successful we are. Defining success, meaning an ideal worth pursuing. Feeling accomplished and being of service to others provides us with the rewards of a healthy lifestyle.

From the moment we get up in the morning, our life is pretty much controlled by our habits, and we don't think. We only *think* when things are outside our habits that we have adapted to over time. If we don't get the results we want, due to our old habits, we need to change, and change isn't easy. It takes thinking and discipline, and often a plan to follow. Habits are not formed overnight, especially good habits. Forming a habit takes more than 60 days, and it all starts with a desire to make a change and drop a habit or create a new one.

I formed a Mastermind Alliance Group some time ago, and we start every morning at 5:00, and we read together on the phone. For me, it was not a big deal, because I had been getting up that early for years, to study, read, or meditate; but for my partners, it was a challenge at first, and they would rely on their alarm clocks to wake them up before 5 a.m. to be on the phone for 5. But because we kept each other accountable, before long, it was something we were all looking forward to, and none of us needed to hear the alarm anymore to get up. If there is a purpose to form a new habit, it's more doable. And when you have someone to keep you accountable, it's easier to keep it up until the habit is formed, and that's after it is required. We all are capable of much more than we ever believe, and it is a matter of knowing what we want, writing it out, and putting action to it. One thing that is vitally important to know is that positive and negative thoughts can't be in your mind at the same time. The thought you give more attention to will dominate. Now that we have set the stage for success, we will see in the following chapters the principles that are vitally important to build a strong financial foundation.

∞ Questions for Success ∞

* What is the most helpful idea from this chapter for you?

* What savings habits were mentioned in this chapter?

* Which person do you identify with the most?

* Which ways of spending do you have that need to change?

Below, write what you want to change in your habits to have the success you want:

1._____

_____

2._____

_____

3._____

_____

4._____

_____

∞ Chapter Three ∞

The Solid Foundation, Step 2

"A sound financial foundation is necessary if a person is to efficiently want to spread goodness to the world."
— Nick Catricala

Proper Protection

Some of us may have had strong community support, where families helped each other out when help was needed. In fact, that is a very good thing to practice. Are you one of those lucky ones who can count on your neighbours, friends, and family when hardship arises and you are in dire need of money? Are you also the one who would willingly give money to someone in need?

I must say, through my own experience, that people are even careful to make friends because of the fear of having to help out; and I don't think it's because people are coldhearted, but it's more because they don't have the extra money to share. It's never easy to admit that we lack money, and a way of avoiding this is to just not commit to be a friend anymore to anyone, just to play it safe.

We have other solutions at hand, so we don't have to expect a friend or relative to pay for our needs. But for some reason, we are still not taking the responsibility to take action.

Most of us are gamblers. This all boils down to lack of understanding, ignorance, procrastination, or even laziness.

Today, so many people think that they can just GO FUND ME on Facebook, and money will come in to take care of their misfortune. It wouldn't surprise me to hear that you are well aware of what I am talking about. Or are you one of those who think that's a good way to get help, or even have been using it?

I am not saying in any way that Go Fund Me is bad, but when I hear opinions or people's attitudes about it, that's what I want to highlight here. If I know what to do, and I don't do it, it's being ignorant. We expect others to give, give, and give, but when the tables turn, we are nowhere to be found.

Look, many of us will insure our cars, our mortgages, our credit cards, our TVs, or our appliances, but have no insurance on ourselves. We insure things that are new and may not break down before they are outdated—like a new TV, a Blu-ray player, a refrigerator, a washing machine and dryer, or a living room set—and none of these things put money into our pockets, yet the most valuable thing we have goes without insurance: Us! Is it not you that brings in the money? Who makes sure that your family has a good lifestyle, and that the bills are paid? Therefore, it's important that you insure yourself.

First, you should have proper disability insurance, and proper health insurance and life insurance in case you die too young, and your family still depends on the money you bring into the household.

It is as much our responsibility to pay for insurance as it is to pay for our cell phone bill, but somehow we cannot come up with the money to pay for insurance; yet we "need" our phones and have to pay. All it is, is instant gratification. We pay for the phone, and we can make a call or text, but when paying for insurance, we often never have to make a claim. And we are fortunate not to, but many, many people do have to, and we know that it could be us one day, sooner or later.

Let me ask you this: If someone in your family had a severe accident or a critical illness like cancer, stroke, heart attack, or any irreversible disease, or you had a family member pass away, who would you be more happy to see—a pastor or friend who prays with you, brings you a card and flowers, and tells you how sorry they are, or an insurance agent who delivers a check that would take care of all the expenses and even beyond? I know the answer. So do you. A prayer is good; in fact, the Bible encourages people to call on others to come and pray for healing, but if you take care of your responsibilities and get protection, you now can really appreciate the pastor, the friend, and the agent, all at the same time.

The following letter is very profound, and I wish I knew who the author was so that I could acknowledge her or him.

Hello!

I am your life insurance policy. You and I have similar purposes in this world. It is your job to provide food, clothing, shelter, schooling, medicine, and other things for your loved ones. You do this while I lie in your safe deposit box. I have faith and trust in you. Out of your earnings will come the cost for my upkeep. At times, I may appear insignificant to you, but someday (and who knows when) you and I will change places.

When you are laid to rest, I will come alive and do your job. I may provide food, clothing, medicine, shelter, schooling, and other things your family will continue to need—just as you are doing now. When your work and labour are done, mine will begin. Through me, your hands can carry on. Whenever you feel the price you're paying for my upkeep is burdensome, remember that I will do more for you and your family than you will ever do for me. If you do your part, I will do mine.

Sincerely yours,
Your life insurance policy

When you go to work, and you have a plan from work, make sure that you also have personal protection outside work as well. Most accidents happen outside the work place, and you wouldn't be covered. A story that I personally was part of, which was not good at all, will tell you why I am saying this.

A couple who were clients of mine were very short on cash flow when I sat down with them to get them protected for life. Both had a compensation from their work place, and their only concern was life insurance. We did apply, and when I suggested to add disability and critical illness insurance to it, the couple declined. I was not comfortable with leaving them without it, but I also knew that it would be tough for them to pay the premium; so, I recommended to take care of that part on my client review date. Before that day came, I got the call that the spouse had gotten into a horrible accident at home and was rushed to the hospital with the STARS. My client went through a 9-hour intense surgery, had multiple minor surgeries, and had ongoing therapies for over a year. Now, not being able to work for so long, and not having personal protection in place, the couple went through lot of hardships, and it was very hard for me to see the struggles in all areas possible. If you don't have proper protection, or you need more information on how that all works, as well as what else you should know about it, go to your financial professional and ask those questions. Don't be afraid of being sold to. Most agents have a big heart to help you understand, and with better understanding, you then can go and make the informed decisions. You also can go on my website, www.YourOwnPayToday.com, to learn more about financial courses that are absolutely free to you, and to have all the topics you need to know on personal finances. Take advantage of them.

I learned from this experience with my clients, to make sure they know how important it is to not wait till the next day, or even longer. It's a horrible feeling when you could've saved someone's future, but you didn't, or you could've done it for yourself but pushed it off. Please don't do that. It's your responsibility, and your family's well-being is at risk. Take action.

Debt Management

How do we go about debt management? Here are some statistics from two of the wealthiest countries in the world: In the USA, student loans surpass $1.5 trillion, and in Canada, it's up to $28 billion, which is $13 billion dollars over what the federal budget is set for. We call this a crisis, which can be defined as an unstable or dangerous event or situation.

Debt on mortgages is even higher. Credit card debt and car loans are higher than ever before.

We have access to debt more than ever before, and we take it. Being able to put 0% down makes it so easy to go and get that car from the lot, which we never would buy if we had to pay in cash. Most don't do the homework and do the math to know what the vehicle will cost in the long run. Not to mention that a car is most likely not an asset, as it will be considered a family or personal vehicle, and not serve as a cab to make money while driving.

Many people blame the government or the economy for the skyrocketing amounts of debt and how it's not managed properly, but we are all responsible to take the time and sit down and work out a budget for our own household.

Would you rather tell your money where to go, or have your money flow away and not know where it went? For some of you, it may be helpful to get someone to help you from the start. I realize that we often put things off when we don't fully understand how to do it or where to start. Go to www.YourOwnPayToday.com, and you will find the support you need. Today, we have no excuses anymore of not having enough information to go by. We are overloaded with information but often don't know where to find reliable information.

Financial Literacy Workshops are held all over Canada and the US, almost every single day. On my website, you can find updated workshop calendars. Check it out and go to them; you can be involved and have your questions answered, and those classes are for educational purposes only.

Harvard University teaches them, and we have them in every province of Canada, and in every state in the USA.

Knowledge is only useful if we apply what we learn, don't you agree? Make sure you find a financial professional who can help you implement what you need, and if you don't know where to go, you can always drop me a question, and I can help you find someone in your area—it doesn't matter if it is the US or Canada. I travel a lot and get to know many people, and I have access to many people. Just ask.

I will give you a short example on debt roll-up, and if you don't have debt problems, just skip this page and move on, or you can help someone you know who would like to learn this concept.

DEBT ROLL-UP

When you follow the illustration, you can see that we start with the smallest amount first, and add only $100 extra on the smallest payment. The rest, we only pay what we have to—the bare minimum. Instead of paying for 18 months on Home Depot, we knock it off in 1.4 months. Now, the 2nd month, we have no Home Depot to pay anymore, so we can now use the same amount we paid last month, and add the extra on the Esso card, which allows us to pay in 5.3 months what would have taken over 26 months, and after the 6th month, we keep following the illustration, and shave many years off of payments, and guess what else? Interest! Bingo, you got it.

Creditors Largest to Smallest	Balance	Minimum Monthly Payment	Roll-Up Payment Amount	Amount of New Payment	# of Remaining Payments	New Pay off
Mortgage	158,400	1,038	1,246	2,284	384.5	147
Bank	30,000	356	890	1,246	120.1	67.4
Car Loan	27,000	530	360	890	58.9	50.4
Mastercard	6,000	100	260	360	311	38.5
Visa	1,500	50	210	260	42	18.8
The Bay	1,200	50	160	210	37	14.4
Sears	700	25	135	160	37	9.4
Esso	525	25	110	135	26	5.3
Home Depot	150	10	100	110	18	1.4
		2,184	100	2,284	29 Years	12.3 Years

This illustration is for educational purposes only, and is not an example that works on the dollar amount at 100%, as interest rates may fluctuate over time, and the amounts could change, but the purpose is to give you an idea, and you now can put in your numbers and take action. That's what counts.

This could save someone from filing for bankruptcy. Never wait when you feel financial stress; seek out professional help sooner than later. It is like a disease or an ulcer: If you don't catch it in the early stage, it gets worse, or it can even lead to a big financial interruption for your family.

Emergency Fund

You may have heard of Murphy's Law...If not, think of it this way. In your unconscious mind are all those thoughts going on that will never shut up. You think with your conscious mind, and when you go to sleep, the part of your mind that stays active is what has filtered into the subconscious mind, and it can be either negative or positive emotions.

The good news is that you can control almost 100% of the emotions that you allow into your subconscious mind.

Here is a list of the seven major positive and negative emotions: (Avoid the negative emotions at all cost.)

Positive Emotions	Negative Emotions
Desire	Fear
Faith	Jealousy
Love	Hatred
Sex	Revenge
Enthusiasm	Greed
Romance	Superstition
Hope	Anger

Why is this important, and what does this have to do with an emergency fund?

Think of this statement: Faith and fear are never found together, and the same thing goes for all the other emotions; you are either in a negative emotion or you are in a positive emotion. The good news is that you can't be in both at the same time, and you can almost have 100% control of what emotion you want to be in.

If you are watching the daily news or listen to it on the radio, you are unconsciously feeding your negative emotions. You are feeding your subconscious mind, all day long, with what the media wants you to feed it, to inject fear of ill health, poor diet, economy downturns, war, disasters, etc. People who live in a state of fear can't prosper. People in a negative state of mind are prone to accidents, and the more you become aware of your state of mind, the more you learn to block negative thoughts and replace them with positive ones.

One very important thing to know is that the negative emotions are injecting themselves through the environment or circumstances, and the positive emotions have to be placed intentionally.

Murphy's Law operates through your state of negative emotions, and brings to you what you fear most. Be careful of your environment, the people you hang out with, and what you are reading or listening to. It all influences your life. It is OK to walk out of a room when people talk about diseases or bad news. Listen, it's all irrelevant anyway, because it's in the past and it doesn't serve us any longer. Why talk about it? Instead, what could we talk about that is positive and could serve to help others, and create good things rather than reliving the past?

I have been studying the mind for close to 15 years, and I know how it affects everything we do, according to what state of mind we are in. Therefore, I always make it top priority to have some sort of savings that are easily accessible, in case I need to pay for something unexpected. This way, I wouldn't have to worry about where the money would be coming from in an emergency, and I could focus on what else I could do to prosper, even though emergencies have never really been an issue in my life.

Savings for an emergency should be in a money market fund that has a low MER and is cashable anytime—not in a locked up GIC. You may not expect that fund to grow much and give you a lot of return money, but you should look for a fund that has the possibility to give you more than inflation cost, so that you won't lose buying power.

In a later chapter, you will learn more about the interest rates and what to look for when you invest your money.

If you don't have an emergency fund, and you think you have a lot of real estate or other assets, remember, an emergency fund should be moneys you can access in a very short time.

How much should we have set aside in an emergency fund? At least 3-6 months of our monthly expenses.

Investments

In the 1940s, we had 40 people working for every 3 people in retirement, and people didn't live as long after age 65. The 401Ks that our southern friends know as a pension plan, or the CPP or RRSP that we have here in Canada, were working for the retiree, but today we have an aging population, and our company pensions or government programs are not working the way they used to. But somehow our whole lifestyle is the same as that of a Baby Boomer's—or maybe even worse? The Baby Boomer got catered to all their life, and most of them had a company pension and got more money from government programs, and they didn't find that they needed to be saving for themselves.

More than ever, people need to change their way of thinking and start saving for themselves to be self secure, instead of relying on the government and thinking the government should take care of their retirement.

We are very lucky in Canada to have government funded health care for general doctor visits, but many people have asked me, what about critical illness treatments and medical tests? Many think that they are all included in the government support, but they are not.

That is why so many people are surprised about the high amount of money we will need in retirement. The average person will need at least a million and half in retirement, but it also depends on where you live. I will add more to this topic in a later chapter. But let me give you a little more detail on polls that CIBC did, and newest stats are from February 2018. They found that a person will need roughly $756,000. Many will need even more.

About 90% of Canadians don't have a plan on how to get there; 53% aren't sure if they are saving enough to reach that goal, and 37% haven't even thought about retirement, or if they have, they don't think they have the money to invest.

Now read this: Only 22% of women have a formal retirement plan, and 32% of men. At the age of 55, 43% of women and 27% of men lack a plan.

The average Canadian has about $144,000, which is still far away from the 3/4 of a million needed. Many fully rely on the Canadian Pension Plan, Old Age Securities, or Guaranteed Income Supplement.

When we look at our American friends across the border, they are not even close to the amount of savings of the average Canadian. Many even think it is OK to default on their mortgages. One out of 6 people say they haven't even thought about retirement planning.

How about you? Have you started your retirement investment plan? Many have lost courage to invest in an RRSP or 401K because of the tax implications when they pull it out. I will show you different ways to allocate your money to spread the risk.

TAX LATER
RRSP/PRIFF
ANNUITIES
RDSP
PENSION
CPP
OAS
RESP
LIRA/LIF

TAX ADVANTAGE
TFSA
PRIMARY RESIDENCE
HEALTH INSURANCE
LIFE INSURANCE BENEFIT
INDIVIDUAL CRITICAL ILLNESS AND DISABILITY INSURANCE

TAX NOW
CHECKING ACCOUNT
SAVINGS ACCOUNT
GIC'S
STOCKS
BONDS
MUTUAL FUNDS
INTEREST INCOME
NON REGISTERED INVESTMENTS

If you allocate your investments in all 3 sections, you have more options to withdraw from, and it can save you thousands of dollars.

Go to my website, www.YourOwnPayToday.com, and check the schedules for the workshops so that you can attend those that you would like to learn more about. On the schedule, you will find a workshop that teaches all about the previous accounts mentioned, and it goes into details. So, check my website for a workshop in your location.

"Being rich is a good thing. Not just in the obvious sense of benefitting you and your family, but in the broader sense. Profits are not a cero sum game. The more you make, the more of a financial impact you can have."
– Mark Cuban

∞ Questions for Success ∞

* What is the most helpful idea from this chapter for you?

* What are the 4 things that we need to know for a strong financial foundation, mentioned in this chapter?

* Have you taken care of all 4 for yourself?

* What are things you should work on as soon as today?

* Below, write what you need to take care of, which has been mentioned in this chapter:

1._____

_____

2._____

_____

3._____

_____

4._____

_____

∞ Chapter Four ∞

The DIME Method, Step 3

For a simple rule of thumb to see how much life insurance you should have, you can use the DIME method. Here is how.

D stands for the amount of debt there is to cover.
I stands for income.
M stands for mortgage.
E stands for education.

According to the Life Insurance and Market Research Association (LIMRA), only 44% of U.S. households have individual life insurance, and the coverage is often not enough. People often say, "I already have life insurance!" They may have some sort of life insurance, but the question is, do they have enough?

It's not good enough to just pick an amount that you think you can afford to pay for. It's important to know how much you need. Then, know what options you have, and pick the right amount for the right price. I will talk more about this later, and show some examples, after we look at cash flow and liabilities.

How would you feel if your $600,000 house burnt to the ground, and when you filed a claim, your insurer told you that you only had $150,000 worth of coverage? That normally wouldn't happen, because the lender wants to make sure you have coverage for the whole amount.

What about for your personal and family needs? If something happens to you and your spouse, and your children make a claim and only receive a small amount, that doesn't leave them with much after all expenses are paid. You are no longer there to provide for them. How would they feel?

The good news with the DIME method is that you can quickly calculate your insurable needs. The bad news is that you may be surprised that you don't have the right amount of insurance.

Cash Flow

I have an entrepreneur family background. My grandparents were farmers, but my paternal grandfather was in trades, construction, and sales. My father farmed, but he also did carpentry and mechanics as a side business.

I must have been in my early teens when my dad talked about careers and having a job or a business. He always said that we should not let it cross our minds to go and work for someone. He said that you should work for yourself and find your passion. He knew that people stop using their full potential when they go to work at a job that pays their bills but has very little meaning to them, so he wanted me and my siblings to use our imagination and be creative—to come up with ideas to earn money to provide for the family.

I think that was one of the greatest gifts we had received from my parents, although I sometimes asked why we should go through all the difficulties that being self-employed brings with it, when you could have a 9-5 job, go to work, have a secure income, and when you get home after 5:00, you can do whatever you want and not have all the worries on your mind that a business can bring with it. I think I was by far not the only person who thought thoughts like that. In fact, some of the people I train in business have those thoughts.

Because of my entrepreneurial upbringing, I don't think I was ever good at having a job. I had a few years of experience working for a boss when I first moved to Canada, in 2009. I needed to establish myself, and I know that those few years, where I made a living working for someone else, have prepared me for what I do now.

The majority of Canadians rely on a job to pay their bills, and businesses need people to work for them. But it will only work if the employee has an interest in what they are doing.

One of my clients really hates his job. I know, that is a strong word, but let me explain. He says, "The moment I clock in at my workplace, I know exactly how many minutes later I will clock out and go home. During my shift, I am on auto pilot, and there is nothing exciting about it. I know exactly how much money I will receive at the end of the pay cycle, and I know where every dollar will go when I receive my pay; and then the next cycle begins, with nothing else other than trading my time for money."

I have asked him a number of times why he remains at that workplace if he dislikes it so much. His answer is: "It pays me well, and I have job security and benefits.

Do you know someone like that? Are you in a situation similar to that?

I teach people to have multiple sources of income. Don't get me wrong. It doesn't mean to have multiple jobs. You only have so many hours a day to exchange your time for money when working at a job or multiple jobs. When you have a business, and are helping people make money, that's when money starts working for you. Now you have not only put in your time but other people's time as well, and there are endless ways that you can do that, but that is a different book to write.

What I want you to learn here is that you need positive cash flow that will pay for all your bills and all your insurances, which will make you able to pay in cash for things, even in a society where using credit is the norm. Cash flow should also help you to be able to fund a good further education fund and retirement. Basically, think of cash flow as money coming to you, be it through employment in your career or through a business, or being self-employed. If you like what you do, congratulations. If it's a job, and you like your job, find something you can do on the side as being self-employed or having a small business while you are working. Why? Let me tell you the brutal truth: Because there is no such thing as secure employment. Period. That is only one reason. If all the money you bring into your household comes from a job, congratulations! You are the biggest tax payer, and the government is your favoured child. Just a thought...

Like I said before, I worked at a job to establish myself when I first moved to Canada, and I could've stayed there until my retirement, had I wanted. I liked what I was doing, and the pay wasn't bad. However, I knew deep in my heart that I had a different calling, and I needed to get on my feet to do more than having a 9-5 mindset. At the same time that I was working, I spent every minute on self-study, and I have taken so many courses that if I were to add them all up, I could have a Ph.D. already.

That may not be something you would like to do, and I am not saying you should, but there is so much more that we can give to the community when we seek beyond what we have been taught in school or can do at a job, to have a fulfilled life.

Liability

What are liabilities?

I absolutely love to work with my young students and trainees who are just starting their lives and getting on their own feet. And working together with my youngest son in the office gave me a lot of opportunities to coach these young people that were his clients. Many of them still had unrealistic dreams, like working at Tim's or Walmart and wanting to retire at age 35. We all know that some bigger moves have to happen before that can happen, but I like the dreaming big part of it. I strongly encourage you to follow your dreams, but put a plan of action in place that will get you there.

Another reason why I like to work with teens and young adults is because they are just starting off, and when we teach them about the money game, and they learn to play it well, they have more time on their side to make a good fortune. Their liabilities are lower, and their debt may be low or they may not have any; although for those pursuing higher education, most of the time, they have a student loan to pay off.

No matter where we are in life, whether we have just started or are close to retirement, we all have to look at what our liabilities are.

Part of proper planning for financial independence is to take an inventory of your money coming in and money going out. In this section, we look at every single dollar leaving our pockets.

One major thing that is overlooked is that you should pay yourself first. Then, give to a charity, and what's left, that's the money you play with.

For very young people, it's often their cell phone bill and some minor spending, but for the young married couple, there are utilities, vehicles, rent or mortgage, groceries, clothing, or even kids and all the expenses that go along with that. For older people, there may be businesses to take into account, or medical expenses. It is always different from person to person, or from household to household. In short, a liability is every expense that takes money out of your pocket.

Now, let me take you to what a plan looks like, considering the X-Factors.

The 10X Factor

I grew up thinking that a person only needed home insurance or vehicle insurance, so that if something happened to the house or to the vehicle, the loss would be replaced by an insurance policy.

No one ever talked about life insurance. Growing up in a third world country, people used cash to buy everything. There was no such thing as using a credit card, or buying something today and paying for it later, on instalments. You only bought what you had cash for, and therefore it was not necessary to have life insurance. When a person passed away, there was no debt to pay or huge liabilities to cover. Although people would have been smart to have life insurance, it was just not talked about, and only rich people would buy life insurance. Not only that, but people would also believe that if they bought life insurance, they could expect to die very soon. Being ignorant is a really funny thing, and it sets people up for failure.

Let me illustrate two case scenarios here. Case scenario number one will talk about a family that has no proper insurance, and case scenario number two will take you to the same family, but with proper coverage.

Case scenario 1

Paul and Maria are a couple with two kids, age 9 and 7.

Both Paul and Maria are working, and their kids are in school.

Paul makes $50,000 a year, and Maria makes $46,000.

They have a mortgage of $250,000.

They have debt of $50,000.

They expect their kids' education to be $120,000.

Paul and Maria believe in putting money away for unexpected expenses, and they work really hard to pay off the debt.

Both have a pension plan at work, where they contribute the maximum, but outside that, they have no savings or investments.

Paul and Maria have heard about insurance, but because they have a pension plan and coverage from work, and a nice income, they don't really think it's necessary to have life insurance. They took the mortgage insurance at their bank, and they think that will take care of everything. They think that paying a premium on a life insurance policy would just be another bill to pay, and they'd rather put that same amount of money towards an education plan for their kids.

Paul and Maria declined a visit from an insurance agent, and told her that they were okay with what they had, and that they had no plans to look into options. They did not want to take the time to spend an hour of their busy lives to sit down and listen to an insurance agent.

Sometime later, Paul started to have severe headaches, and he went to the doctor to see what was wrong. After some tests, the doctor informed the couple that a brain tumour had been found, and that there was nothing they could do. A couple of months later, Paul passed away.

Maria is on her own now, with her kids, and finds that the bills are too high for just one income. She is happy that the mortgage insurance paid out, and that she has no mortgage anymore and can stay with her kids in the house. But she has to find someone to take care of her kids while she's at work, and that is another expense. She stops putting money away for the kids' higher education so that she can pay for a babysitter while she is at work, when the kids are not in school. She even takes on a second job, but she feels bad about being away from home so much, and hardly ever sees her kids. But what else can she do? She is responsible for her kids, and that's what counts. She finds that life is hard, and she is always tired, but work never stops, and she won't be able to send her kids to university or college. They will have to work and go to school at the same time.

Case scenario 2

Paul and Maria agreed to sit down with Teresa, an insurance agent, to have her look over their insurance needs.

They have the same amount of income, the same mortgage amount, and the same debt, and they expect the same amount for the kids' higher education.

The insurance agent explains mortgage insurance versus personal insurance, and Paul and Maria decide to apply for personal insurance, but how much should they have?

Teresa writes down all the numbers of their income, liabilities, savings, and RESP contributions. Then she explains that after expenses, the couple is left with $320, discretionary money that they can use to put a proper plan in place.

Teresa is using the DIME method to quickly calculate the amount needed. She explains the 10X factor and the 20X Factor.

Paul needs $920,000.

Maria needs $880,000.

Paul and Maria decide to apply for a simple Term 20, applying the 10X Factor. They will have paid off their house by then, and the kids will have left the house and most likely be finished school by that time.

Teresa wants to make sure that the kids are protected as well. She explains that the cost of insurance for the kids is low, and that they can take the policy over once they have a job and can keep paying their own premium.

Paul and Maria are happy that Teresa takes the time to explain different options, and they decide to take a whole life policy of $250,000 for both their kids.

They will continue their personal savings plan for unexpected expenses.

Paul and Maria are very excited when the policies are approved, and they go to their bank and cancel the mortgage insurance because they no longer need it, and don't want to pay the extra premium.

Sometime later, Paul started to have severe headaches, and he went to the doctor to see what was wrong. After some tests, the doctor informed the couple that a brain tumour had been found, and that there was nothing they could do. A couple of months later, Paul passed away.

Maria and the kids were devastated about the loss of Paul, and Maria was also concerned that the insurance may not pay out because not even a year had passed since they had applied. Teresa, the insurance agent, had told them about the incontestable period of 2 years after the policy came in force. However, no evidence was found that Paul had the tumour before they applied, and Teresa got the check for $920,000 from the insurance company.

Teresa sat down with Maria one more time, and Maria was now able to put money into an investment account for her kids' further education. She paid up the premium for her kids' policy, converted her own policy into a layered universal life policy, and made arrangements at her bank to pay off the rest of the mortgage and clear all the debt that was left.

She opened a TFSA for herself and maxed it out, and put the rest of the money into a segregated investment.

Maria wants to spend more time with her children now, as that is all she has left for family after Paul's passing She applied for a part time position at her job so that she would not have to work full time any longer. That would allow her to be out and about, giving her some time to be among people and not just by herself at home while the kids are in school. She likes her job, but this way she can be home when the kids get home from school.

You can see the huge difference it makes for a family when there is proper protection in place and someone passes away. We don't get second chances like Paul and Maria did, and therefore, we need to take action while we still can.

I didn't get into talking about critical illness insurance, personal disability, or long- term care. My point here is to illustrate the impact that proper protection has, and how the 10X Factor allowed Maria to not only have her mortgage paid off but to have so many other things taken care of at the same time.

The 20X Factor

If we factor in the 20X Factor, it is a whole different way of structuring a policy. We times the annual income by 20 instead of 10 like we did with the 10X Factor.

The reason we use the 20X Factor is to fund our retirement through an insurance policy, and there are different ways to do that. I won't go into details here, other than pointing back at the different ways of allocating your money for the purpose of tax implications, which I mentioned in the previous chapter.

Preparing for a long retirement needs a long time for your investment to grow, and people often don't have that much time left. Many don't even start to save for their own retirement until after the kids have finished school, and a much larger amount is needed to start off with to recoup the missing amount.

A UL life insurance policy, if properly structured and funded, can help, and there are a few options to look into, using an indexed annuity or a guaranteed money withdrawal benefit policy with a floor.

If you need an expert in this field, look for someone who has the heart of a teacher and will explain to you in simple words about the options, and who will help you make informed decisions to make your money work for you.

Also, you can go to www.YourOwnPayToday.com, and ask for help to find a trusted expert in your area, that I can endorse.

Education Fund

In Canada, most people know that they can save for their kids' education through an RESP. Very few understand the program though, and often people are surprised when they don't get all the grants that they expected when they started the plan. One reason could be that the kid is not going to an approved university for the plan, or it's not a family plan, where the sibling or parent can use the money if one kid goes to a college or university that is not approved in the plan.

Go to www.YourOwnPayToday.com, and subscribe to my newsletter; learn all the details of an RESP so that you understand the details.

There are also ways to prepare for kids' further education through a life insurance policy, and it may be a good thing to have both an RESP and a whole life or universal life insurance policy for your kids. You have much more flexibility through and insurance policy than through an RESP, but you get some free money from the government when you open an RESP for your kid. It is always good to know your options, and to use what works in your best interest.

Your FIN

I have talked before about the 20X Factor, and I want to bring it up here again because it is important for our *FIN* number. (Financial Independence Number).

What is your age today?

How much savings do you have?

How many years till you want to retire?

What is your approximate life expectancy?

In today's dollar, how much do you expect your monthly living expenses to be in retirement?

Now, if you factor in inflation of 3-4%, you can calculate what your monthly living expenses will be by the time you retire. Multiply that by 20, and subtract the amount of savings you already have, and the answer will be the amount needed. Now, divide that amount in the months till your retirement, and run different scenarios of compounding interest rates that will outpace inflation, and you will know how much money you should save on a monthly basis.

Always factor in taxes and inflation.

I run these numbers all the time with my clients. We need to know what that FIN number looks like so that we can plan accordingly.

In many cases, people don't see themselves retiring at all when they see the amount of money they will need. That's why it's so important to plan and use strategies that can support you to reach the desired goal.

In the next chapter, I will explain more about what strategies you can use.

∞ Questions for Success ∞

* What is the most helpful idea from this chapter for you?

* What does 10X Factor stand for?

* Have you applied the 20X Factor when you applied for life insurance?

* Name at least 2 different options for kids' further education funding.

* Below, write what you need to take care of while you still can:

1._____

_____

2._____

_____

3._____

_____

4._____

_____

∞ Chapter Five ∞

The X-Curve, Step 4

I will explain here about the X-Curve concept.

It symbolizes how to build wealth with responsibility.

It is a simple concept and illustrates the relationship between taking care of your responsibility and building wealth at the same time.

Over time, as you pay off debts and have more savings, your wealth increases and your responsibility decreases.

When You Are Younger

Let's take a look at Paul and Maria again.

Paul and Maria are a newly married couple, and they have a conversation about what they should do from the start to build wealth over time and take care of their responsibilities from the get-go. They decided to give me a call to set up an appointment.

When I met with Paul and Maria, they told me that they wanted to do the right things with their finances, but they didn't understand many things, as they had never learned about it in school, and their parents had never really talked much about finances.

They have some friends with whom they talk about finances and money, but no one really understands what to do or how it all works, and they had a lot of questions. I took the time to listen to them.

I asked them about their goals and their dreams, and they told me that they wanted to buy a house in the next couple of years.

They also would like to travel once in a while, and would like to eventually start a family once they're more settled.

Both still have a student loan to pay off, and they bought a car that was financed at their bank.

They have not started an emergency fund yet, and they have no protection whatsoever.

After they shared all this with me, they wanted to know what would be in their best interest to do with their financial plan.

I handed them some forms to start a budget, and showed them how to use it. They asked me if they could make copies of them so that they could have one for the following month. Of course, I told them that was a great idea.

Both Paul and Maria make a good income and, so far, they put every single dollar towards the student loans to pay them off quickly.

Like Paul and Maria, taking responsibility from the get-go is important, but we all know that we have to eventually start wherever we are, and make the best we can out of it.

Going back to Chapter 3, I explained the financial foundation. Let's take a look how we can apply that to Paul and Maria's plan.

We calculated their current and future life insurance needs (disability and critical illness coverage for both).

We looked at their total debt amount and started a strategy for payments to pay it off in the shortest possible time. We calculated in a mortgage amount, if they were to buy a house, and what amount of money they would need to furnish it, as well as some monies to get away on a short vacation once in a while.

We calculated how much money they could save into their emergency fund, and opened a mutual fund. They want to take advantage of the dollar-cost averaging (DCA) way of investing. So, we set up the plan that after each pay, a little amount of money would be withdrawn from the investment company of their choice, as automatic withdrawals, which not only gives them peace of mind that they won't forget about it, but also starts the habit of saving.

We calculated their FIN number, and I ran a few illustrations for them, using investments and insurance to get to their desired goal.

Now that they had a good understanding of what the numbers look like, we could start building their plan.

I put a plan together for life insurance, disability, and critical illness, so that they are safe in the case of a disability or critical illness while they are working. Should one of them die soon, the surviving spouse would be able to continue on, clear all debt, and possibly take some time off from work to travel and/or get their life back on track after the grieving.

We opened up an RRSP account for both of them, where they will start to invest, also using the dollar-cost averaging strategy, and paying into each account half of what their future mortgage would be. This will start the habit of living without the amount of money that they otherwise would pay for their mortgage, and it also will enable them to save for the down payment, with some interest, and they will get a refund the following year on their tax filing, which they can put towards some furniture.

First, Paul and Maria were a little bit concerned that they wouldn't be able to pay off their student loans so quick if they now had all these other areas to put their money towards, but we were able to make a little bit more than the minimum payments required, and Paul offered to pick up a few extra hours at his job and put the extra money towards his student loan, and Maria said she could do the same.

For the life insurance, they decided that they wanted to take a universal life policy so that they could start, at the same time, to build up wealth for retirement. I explained to them that they needed to be disciplined with the plan so that the plan would work for them, and according to the illustration, and if they keep up their side of the contract, they would have close to $1.5 million, accessible at the age of 65.

Both seemed to be very excited about their plan, and they wanted to take advantage of the Financial Literacy Workshops, so I handed them a schedule with the times and location.

After each workshop, we will go over their questions so that they can really take control of their financial situation, with great understanding.

I meet with Paul and Maria 2-3 times a year, and they always have more questions for me. They not only took the workshops once, but they came back for the second time, and they now have a good understanding of all the concepts and strategies.

Paul and Maria bought their dream house a few years ago, using their RRSPs for the down payment, and taking advantage of the First Time Home Buyers Plan.

They have 3 beautiful children, and they decided to fund their kids' further education through whole life insurance instead of using an RESP plan. They make the payments from the Child Tax Benefit they get every month, and when the kids get money on their birthdays or such, they put it into a savings account to teach their kids at an early age to save, invest, and not spend it all.

When You Are Older

Maria and Paul are empty nesters now. The kids are off to university, and their mortgage is paid off. They have no debt, and they start to travel more often.

You see? With proper planning, they are financially independent now. It was not easy for them, and a lot of discipline was needed; often, it seemed like they would have to take on a line of credit to make ends meet, or look for more income, especially during the time when Maria stayed home when their kids were born. But because they learned discipline from the get-go, they pulled it off; and today, they are so happy they did.

This scenario worked out well, and you may think, "I wish I had started this way when I was young, but now there is not much I can do."

Well, you are right; it would be ideal if everyone would start off strong, but the most important thing you can do is to learn how money works. Once you understand the *money game*, you can apply those rules everywhere. Start today—the "what if's" don't serve us, and the best we can do is take action.

The scenarios given here are for the purpose of education only; each individual case is different and needs to be customized accordingly.

A universal life insurance policy is not good for everyone; neither is a term insurance policy ideal for everyone, or a whole life policy. You need understanding first, before you make your final decisions.

When You Die Too Soon

When we take a look at what would have happened if Paul had died at age 30, we would see that Maria could pay off all their debt and their mortgage. She could keep the same lifestyle but maybe stop working, staying home with the kids, helping out with volunteering here and there, or whatever the case may be. She would feel safe and stress-free because she would not be concerned about her finances.

If Maria had died at age 30, Paul could have done the same, paying off all the debt and the mortgage, and most likely staying at home with the kids as long as he needed, or until they were old enough to go to college or university, and he could pick up a job or even start a business for himself.

Less than a year ago, I got notified that a close friend of mine, back in Mexico where I come from, was admitted to the hospital with pneumonia.

First, none of us thought that it was as serious as it turned out to be, but after only about a month later, he passed away.

As an insurance agent, it is my duty to make people aware of their insurance needs, because it can save their families' futures. But this couple lived in Mexico, and I don't carry an insurance license for Mexico. I could not have personally helped him with insurance, but I could have made them aware of what they should own, and they could have found it through an insurance agent in their area.

I had mentioned before that we don't talk about life insurance in Mexico, although more and more people have started to see the importance of having life insurance. My friends did not have any protection other than health insurance.

When my friend told me that her husband was admitted to the hospital and was really sick in the ICU, I asked her if they had critical illness insurance or life insurance; and sadly, she said, "No Katharina," we don't have anything. She then asked me, "Can you please help us get insurance?" But at this time, it was too late. I had to tell her that I couldn't send anyone who would be able to insure her husband right now, because he was sick in the hospital. I told her that they could hope for the best, and if he got well again, they should definitely look into getting proper protection as soon as possible. But right then, I couldn't do anything for them.

It was not that this couple had no monies, because they had businesses; but all the money was sitting in the business, and the cash flow was tight. The lady was now going through a very stressful time because of that. Had I told them about their insurance needs, and that they should look to find an agent in their community to get them protected, I would have helped them big time; but now I am mourning with them, with the regret of not having told them.

I don't want that to happen to you, and I encourage you, wherever you are, to go and find someone in your area that can help you put protection in place, so that you don't have to go through a stressful time when the worst things happen.

I do not carry any licenses in the US, but I am licensed in

many provinces across Canada. I can help you, or I can find someone for you if you don't have an agent to reach out to. Don't wait till it's too late.

When You Live Too Long

How will it look for Paul and Maria if they grow old together and are in their mid-70s now?

We had set up their plan when they were young, and their plan grew over the years, to the point that they did not need any insurance anymore because they now had a lot of savings.

The X curve worked perfectly fine for them. When they were younger, they were covered for their liabilities, and their savings plan had time to grow over the years.

When they got older, they did not have as many liabilities, and we dropped more and more insurance, but their investment still kept growing.

Now they can use their investments from inside the universal life policy to cover their monthly expenses, or for travel, or for whatever their needs are; and they don't have to just rely on their pension plan or an RRSP. Paul and Maria pay very little taxes now, if at all, because they have different areas where they can take money from, and it is not all taxable income.

As I mentioned in Chapter 3, many people are not prepared for retirement, and many don't even know how to get there. Many have not even given it a thought, or they believe that they don't have money to invest at all.

What is your situation? Do you have a proper plan in place that covers you now, while you have liability, or that will add up to your retirement plan when you get older? I hope you have seen the importance, in the last chapters, of what it means to be protected, and also what it means to plan for retirement.

Many people have all their assets in their family home, in real estate, or in a business. And many will have to dissolve their assets to have enough money to cover their expenses in retirement. Long-term care is definitely something that people start to be concerned about more and more as we get into a more ageing population, and we see people living to an older age but not having saved accordingly during their working years.

Many families define themselves as the sandwich generation: a couple who needs to take care of their growing kids as well as take care of their ageing parents.

You can imagine that there is very little money left for themselves, or even to put money away for their own retirement while they are still working.

Where does that take us?

How can we do better?

Is it time that we get more educated on the game of money?

We live in a different world today than 50 years ago, where pension plans were the norm, and people could retire with the government's support and their pension plan. Today, retirement has become a crisis, and we are not prepared to take care of the ageing population in the way they should be taken care of.

Resident care homes are always full, and they all have a long waiting list, which means that the parents have to stay with the kids or in the hospital if they need special care until a spot opens in a care home.

Do the parents have the money to pay for the cost of a care home or for private care at home? Many don't, and this won't get any better if we don't take control and start putting money away for our own retirement.

We should look into a long-term care insurance policy while we are young, or at whatever age we are, because most likely we will need it one day—and again, don't wait till it is too late.

The X-Curve is meant to take care of your financial needs when you are young and have a lot of financial responsibilities. As you grow older, and your liabilities are less and less, it gives you peace of mind with the wealth that has built up over the years. And if you die too soon, your family can move on without financial interruptions; and if you live a long life, you will have savings to take care of you.

∞ Questions for Success ∞

* What is the most helpful idea from this chapter for you?

* Are your financial affairs in order in case you die too soon?

* Have you prepared to be fine if you live a long life?

* What does the X-Curve represent to you?

* Below, write what you need to take care of while you still can:

1._____

_____

2._____

_____

3._____

_____

4._____

_____

∞ Chapter Six ∞

The Law of Giving, Step 5

"We make a living by what we get;
we make a life by what we give."
- Winston S. Churchill

Why is Giving Important?

For what occasions do we think of giving? Birthdays? Holidays? Bridal showers? Baby showers? Charities? Communities? Donations to the Red Cross, MCC, the Salvation Army, or any different foundations?

I remember that I would give part of my allowance to my Sunday school class, where we collectively gathered monies to donate to people who needed financial help. We would prepare shoe boxes with school supplies for kids in the Sierra Madre, and the ladies would add clothes and blankets for the families, to keep them warm in the cold winter months in the far copper canyons.

Giving goes way back in history where God commanded the Israelites to give a tenth to the temple. And long before we read about it in the Bible, Abraham gave a tenth to Melchizedek, the king of Salem.

Why giving? I remember that my life coach, Bob Proctor, would explain it this way: If you have something in your hand, and you hold on to it and are afraid to lose it, it prevents you from getting more. But when you open your hand in a giving way, you are also able to receive.

I have observed many people over my lifetime, who were gracious givers, and how their life was blessed. When we give, it triggers joy to come into our hearts, and it's not always monetary how we get the blessings back through giving, but we have a healthier, joyful life.

Look at the farmer; he plants seeds in the ground, and out of one seed grows 30, 50, or even 100 more seeds. The law of nature teaches us abundance.

Giving teaches us faith, according to Dr. Napoleon Hill's third step towards riches, in his book, *Think and Grow Rich*.

Giving brings joy to our life. When we give, we share, and we care. I encourage you to give in abundance and experience the blessings that come out of giving.

You may say that you will give once you have money, but think of giving in this way: You don't sit in front of the fireplace and say, "Give me heat and I will give you firewood." No, you give the wood first, to receive the heat.

I learned a long time ago to pay myself first before I paid anyone else; and I had the money automatically come out of my bank account and go into my long-term investments before I would pay any bills, do any shopping, or spend any money. I soon realized that I could live off of less than my full paycheck. I also wrote post-dated checks to my charity of choice for a whole year. Even though I was on straight commission and did not have a secure salary, I was always able to pay for my monthly expenses. I am not saying this to impress you but to demonstrate that when we act out of faith, and give, we get. Many a life has been touched by someone who gives.

Giving does not mean only monetarily. We can give our time to help someone. We can give our expertise or our talents. Often, it is easier for us to write a check and give it to a charity than to actually show up and put our time and effort into the need. For some, it may be easier to volunteer with giving time instead of money. It is still giving, and it all counts to make this world a better place.

How Much Should I Give?

Through my work, I meet people from all walks of life and all types of religions. Some are devoted to tithe 10 per cent, and others give what they feel they can afford.

I am not telling you how much you should or shouldn't give, but let me shed some light on the amount, from experience, be it from my personal giving or from what my clients share with me.

We have seen, in Chapter 3, the importance of building and having a solid financial foundation. That is the single most important thing to do. Without proper protection, our savings can blow out the window overnight, and we could find ourselves getting into debt. Our long-term investments could shrink from day to day. When we take care of that responsibility, we can focus on other things.

I have had clients tell me that even though their cash flow is extremely tight, they are obligated to give 10 per cent to their church organization, or that they think they need to give in order to receive. If we give with the thought in mind that we will receive 10 times what we give, or according to how much we give, it robs us of the blessings that we get when we give with a cheerful heart without expecting anything in return. Giving should never be forced, and it should always be in faith that it will provide blessings to the receiver and the giver.

Sometimes we feel obligated to give when we see that the need is so huge, and I know, on occasions when I have given more than I felt I could, I made it through the next month, and my faith just got stretched.

I believe in giving and in giving generously, but our first responsibility is to provide food, clothing, and shelter for our loved ones. How much, depends on how much you feel you can give, and acting in faith is a marvelous thing that will teach you many lessons in life. If we only give from our discretionary money, we will miss out on growth.

Did you know that a life insurance policy can be used to give money to an organization? Yes, you heard me right. When you don't need the proceeds from the life insurance payout for final expenses, and your family is well taken care of, you can make a church or an organization the beneficiary of your policy, to receive a lump sum, or you can even have them purchase a life annuity or a term annuity to provide instalments of payouts to happen over a long time. In this case, you can give much more than you possibly ever could while you were alive.

Who Should You Give To?

I have always been blessed with a church community that ran many projects where money was needed to cover the expenses, and missionary work that was of huge blessings. When I gave my money for the church offering, I felt that the people in charge of that money did a great job of distributing it so that nothing would get thrown to places or projects where I wouldn't want it to go, and I basically did all my tithing and offering through my church. I don't like it when solicitors come to my door and ask me to sponsor a child or to give to a certain charity of their choice, because I have no idea if the money is really going to where it is supposed to.

We can give to organizations where our dollar will become 2 dollars, by businesses or organizations matching the amount, or when we get a tax refund for dollars we have donated, and we give it back, to give the following year.

We may have experienced difficulties in our lives, where a charity has helped us out, and we believe now in the good deeds that charity does, and we make it our charity to give to.

I just want you to know that you should do your research as to what you give, so that you know the money you donate is well invested in things that you approve of.

What about the $1.00 you can donate when you buy something at Walmart, and they have the option to donate for whatever cause? Again, in my opinion, you have to do your research before you give that $1.00.

Should we give to the beggars on the streets? I may get into hot water with my statement, but I don't really care. What I think we do when we give them money is enable them to be lazy, and if it's not that, it may be that the person who is collecting the money is not even the receiving party. Let me explain: I lived in Mexico for almost 40 years, and we had people begging for money at just about every traffic light in the city. It was often a challenge for the driver to not drive over someone running out into the street. Those people begging all day for money on the street actually walked away with more money at the end of the day than the person who worked all day in a factory. Even worse, in many cases, we witnessed where a person would drop off a bunch of poor people, with a very nice pickup truck in the morning, and then pick them up in the late afternoon, take all the money from the people, and give them a few lousy pesos for begging all day. It worked like the black market where human trafficking was practiced, and these poor people stayed poor while the rich took advantage of the "slaves," which is what I would call it in this case.

I have a heart for helping those people on the street, but I don't believe it's a solution to poverty when we give them money on the street. People should not have to do that.

I also have experienced, on many occasions, where ladies would come to my door begging for something to feed their kids, and sometimes there was a legitimate poor person asking for help; but many times, they would ask for money, and when I offered them food or clothes instead, they would refuse to take it, or it would get thrown away on the street. People needed money to purchase street drugs or smokes.

It is best that you check what the money will go towards, and do your research. Sometimes people are in real need, and we have given to the right person who really got blessed by it. It's not my opinion that you should go by but what your heart is telling you.

Is Tithing and Offering the Same?

When we tithe, we give from our first amount, which we give as a gift to the receiver of our donation, but our offering is from the money we have set aside for daily living expenses. It's like providing the money for the church budget to pay the bills, like hydro, cleaning, internet and phone service, etc., whereas tithing is going to service the community, missionary works, hospitals, schools, different organizations who do charitable works, etc.

When we give only our tithing and nothing to the offering, it is like paying ourselves first but defaulting on our household bills.

Benefits of Giving

The benefits of giving will vary from case to case and from person to person, but when we cheerfully give, we do ourselves a great service. We are healthier and happier, and we are blessed by the great feeling we get when we give.

We may have helped angels when we gave. We may have saved a family from losing everything they had, or we might have just given someone hope for another day. We often won't see the results in our lifetime, but knowing that we helped someone in need will bring a huge blessing to us.

Another huge benefit of giving is that we stretch our faith, and we can apply that to personal growth and become a stronger person.

∞ Questions for Success ∞

* What is the most helpful idea from this chapter for you?

* Are you a cheerful giver?

* What is tithing?

* What is offering?

* Below, write down where you like to give your money.

1._____

_____

2._____

_____

3._____

_____

4._____

_____

∞ Chapter Seven ∞
The Rule of 72, Step 6

The Formula

My father was the very first person who introduced me to the rule of 72, and I understood the concept but only learned about the formula later on. I can't recall having seen it in school, and if we had it, I can't remember.

It is a concept that is so powerful! But only few make the effort to expand the teaching on it. To make this statement sink in a little bit more, let me share a little story here. When I was in my first year in financial services, I needed to see my banker and booked an appointment with him, and when I entered his office, I noticed on his wall a framed certificate of his completion as a securities licensed representative. I told him that I carry the same license, and he wanted to know more about where I work and my book of assets under management. Somewhere I had mentioned the rule of 72, and he looked at me with a puzzled look on his face, asking me what I meant by the rule of 72. Now it was my turn to look puzzled at him, the *banker*, asking me that question. He wanted to know more, and he asked me if he could come to my financial service centre and sit down with me, because he realized that he was missing some very important facts.

Often, we think that going to our banker, and having all our financial affairs taken care of at our local branch, will be all we need to have our money work for us, but I want you to look at it this way: If you go to your dentist, she will take care of your dental health but will know very little about heart surgery, and definitely would not know what to do if you needed spectacles, or how to treat pancreas problems. The same goes for the banker; he is trained to service the client with what they can offer you at their branch, and they are good at it, but when it comes to your holistic financial plan, they cannot service you in all aspects. Number 1, they don't have the tools, the licenses needed, or access to the financial plans needed to build your plan that will work for you if the market goes up or down or sideways. They only can service you with the products and services they have at their local branch. Number 2, banks are there to make money with our money, and when you know the *formula* of the rule of 72, and you divide 72 by the interest rate the bank offers you, you will have the answer to how long it will take for your money to double. You also will see that you won't get anywhere close to where you could just knowing and understanding the *formula*.

Let me give you a few hypothetical examples of how the rule of 72 works:

Divide 72/4=18. If you get 4% compounding interest on your investment, your money will have doubled in 18 years, but maybe it's just barely outpacing inflation. Is that good enough? Do you get 4% where you have your money invested?

Now, divide 72/8=9. At 8% compounding interest, your investment will double in 9 years. You do the math on your investment, with the interest rate you get and the age you are.

Will your investment grow to the amount you need? How about if you get 12%?

It's not only the interest rate you need to look at when investing; there is much more to it, and I will explain the different types of interest later in this chapter. For now, I just want you to do some calculations on your desired amount of money needed to retire and pay for your needs.

Compounding Interest

As I had mentioned before, it's important to know the difference between linear interest and compounding interest.

Linear interest:

If you invest $10,000 at 8 per cent over a year, you would have made $800. You take the $800 in cash, pay the capital gains tax on it, and keep investing your $10,000 for another year, and pull out the cash from the interest you get. Very simple, right?

Compounding interest:

You invest $10,000 at 8 percent over a year. You receive $800 in interest, and you don't cash it out. Instead, it's added to your initial investment; and now, in the second year, not only does your capital generate you interest, but the interest you got last year is growing now at 8%. If it's in a tax deferred account or a segregated investment, you don't pay taxes on the capital gains until you cash it out, and that will also allow you to grow the full amount to a bigger amount over the years.

These are hypothetical examples for illustration purposes, but it definitely will give you an idea of what the difference is between linear and compounding interest.

It's very important that you know how to read a financial statement, but you should not hesitate to reach out to a licensed financial professional if you don't understand. We don't learn these things in school, and we often read articles that have all these difficult terms that we don't understand, and we end up confusing people more than actually helping them to understand. Reach out for help, and learn the game of money. It's your money at the end of the day, and no one is more interested in your money than you are; therefore, you should know what is in your best interest so that you can do better.

Bypassing the Middleman

My ex-husband and I had an apple orchard in Mexico, and growing the apples was quite similar to growing money. We had to work the soil, and test the soil and the leaves on a regular basis to prevent diseases and to make sure that the soil had all the minerals, calcium, vitamins, and nitrogens needed to grow a healthy crop. There were a lot of expenses involved with that, and a constant observation and maintaining to finally pick the apples, package them, and sell them on the market.

To sell the apples, we had to go through the middleman, sell them for whatever the market price was at the time of harvest, and just hope all year long that China or the USA wouldn't overflow the market and push the prices down.

Although my ex-husband used future selling or options, he still depended on the person buying the apples from our yard and distributing them to the markets in Guadalajara or Mexico City, and that person usually made the bigger share of gain than we did with a whole year of putting work into it.

We can easily compare this with a GIC at our local bank branch that pays us a low interest rate of 1% or not even. Dividing 72 into 1 doesn't look to me like making money at all, but it is more like our money is just sitting in the bank over the years until we have access to it, or like someone turning around and lending us a mortgage at 3 plus %, or a line of credit for over 5%, or even worse, a credit card for 19.99%. Yes, your money is working for someone, but not for you! Not even a chance.

What about taking a look at different ways of investing your money? Please read on...

Be Your Own Money Manager

Do you know that you can be your own money manager? There are different ways of investing and growing your money. I am not referring here to anything "get-rich-quick." Stay away from investments you don't understand and which promise you extremely high rates of return in a very short time. If you are a sophisticated expert in reading charts and studying the markets, this is not the message for you. You could do well there, but if you are not that person, be careful with your money. There are safer ways and good opportunities over a long period of time to make your money grow.

What do I mean by being your own money manager, if I suggest you stay away from taking the risk of high returns on your money?

You have to understand that with higher returns, there is also a higher risk involved, and it's not a given to time the markets. But let me show you one example that has made a lot of money for my clients, and that you can use for yourself as well.

Dollar-cost averaging:

This is a way of investing that is good for those who want to get into the habit of saving. You can put small or large amounts of money into an investment, on a weekly, bi-weekly, or monthly basis, directly out of your checking account from your bank. You have the advantage to buy units/shares for low prices, and later sell them for a higher price. Because you buy often, you buy more units when the market goes down, and you can watch when they are more expensive, when you need to sell.

This is also a good way to keep buying units and leave the investment for the long term.

Being your own money manager simply means that you go directly to an investment company to pick the funds you want to invest in. Have a licensed representative show you your best suitability options and set it up for you.

Pay Yourself First

If you are self-employed, working for a salary, or own a business, you should consider to give 10% away, like I mentioned before in the chapter on giving.

The next 10% should go to yourself—not to spend it but to invest. Like I mentioned before, in dollar-cost averaging, this can be the money that you could invest that way. Every time you get paid, a certain amount gets deposited into your investment. This is now considered investing for retirement, or to have money saved for an opportunity that could come along.

Warren Buffet used to say: *"Save first, and spend what is left after savings."*

Consider investing, and all that I have written about saving and investing, as things from the past, because we don't know what will happen tomorrow—whether we will have disasters strike; what food supplies we will have; or where technology will take us. Changes always happen, and by the fact alone that we save small amounts of money, may not be too encouraging for you, and it's definitely not the only way we should look at to build wealth, but it can be of great contribution and more than we realize at first—small things can make a huge difference. I would rather have as much savings as I can in investments, not knowing what the future return on my money will be, than to not having anything saved at all.

Bonus at www.YourOwnPayToday.com:
Find an illustration on dollar-cost averaging.

∞ Questions for Success ∞

* What is the most helpful idea from this chapter for you?

* How can you apply the rule of 72 to your advantage?

* Do you save first and spend what's left, or do you intend to save after spending?

* Why should you save?

* Do you pay yourself first?

Write down a few things that you are saving money for:

1._____

_____

2._____

_____

3._____

_____

4._____

_____

∞ Chapter Eight ∞

Budgeting, Step 7

Total Income

When I collect data from my clients to do a financial needs analysis for them, the total amount of income is the easiest to know. People know how much money they make, bi-weekly, in a month, quarterly, or annually.

The problem often is that we don't understand the different types of income.

I mean, we know how much money is coming in, but is it earned income, capital gain, dividends, CPP, OAS, or other? It's where we need to understand that not all money is taxed the same; and another thing, the child tax money is not an income. It shouldn't go straight into the financial budget as if it were earned income.

Why do we need to know where the money is coming from? Because of tax purposes.

It's not how much money you make but how much you keep that counts.

You want to make sure that there is more money coming into your household than going out. But then you also want to make sure that you keep as much money in your pocket as possible. Therefore, it's important to know what kind of investment you have, how it's invested, and what your money can do for you.

You should go to a professional to have these conversations, and work closely together to get the best possible out of your money. It is also important that you look for help from someone who can offer you a whole financial plan, starting with financial education, and also being able to use everything for your financial planning so that you don't have to go to 3 or 4 different advisors to take control over your financial future. Knowing less can cost more.

Total Expenses

If you are the person who has a budget, it will be an easy task for you to do an analysis. I find though, for many people, it's not the case. For many, it will be the first time.

Many people have only 1 or 2 income streams, and many areas where the money is going. The important thing is that you know where it's going and keep close track of it. If you don't tell your money where to go, it will go where it wants to. Remember, money doesn't sleep, and it's liquid—it flows. It never stands still.

If you give to charity, and pay yourself first, you have taken care of two very important things. How much do you have left after you give, and after you pay yourself?

Most North Americans spend 70 more cents on a dollar than they earn. Now, how is that possible? It may be beneficial to us if that wouldn't be possible. We wouldn't buy the things with money we don't have, to impress people who don't care. Don't you agree?

We have our house on a mortgage, access to money through credit cards and lines of credit, student loans, and car loans. We may not have a dollar left in our checking account, but we can swipe the card or pull from the overdraft protection. That's how we are able to spend almost double the amount we make.

Life can happen to us, and we can face challenging times, but most of us are active spenders and passive savers—don't you agree?

Our regular bills should not be more than the money we earn. We all know that we need a positive cash flow to get ahead in life and to build up wealth for retirement, and that we need to force ourselves into more savings, which on the other hand is not possible if we have too little positive cash flow.

When you write down all your monthly expenses for 3 months, it will give you a pretty accurate number of the amount of money you need for your monthly spending. I encourage you to do that. You can go to my website and find printable budgeting forms that will help you as a guide. Soon you will realize that by writing things down in regard to where your money is going, it will save you a lot of money. Give it a try for at least 3 months.

Write Your Own Paycheck

Some ideas on how to divide the budget into percentages:

- Charitable gifts: 10%-15%
- Pay yourself: 10%-12%
- Utilities: 5%-10%
- Housing: 25%-35%
- Clothing: 2%-7%
- Recreation: 4%-10%
- Personal: 5%-10%
- Food: 5%-15%
- Debt services: 10%-15%
- Medical: 1%-2%
- Transportation: 10%-15%
- Emergency: 5%-10%

Just consider, if you make a quarter million a year, these percentages are way off. I don't think you want to spend $25,000 on your grocery bill; you would be rather wide and bulky. You get my point. This is more of a guideline on an average income.

Education Fund

We don't know what we don't know, and when it comes to money issues, believe me, I meet with people all the time who are telling me again and again, "I didn't know that," or "Why didn't we learn this in school?"

We have a lot of immigrants in North America, and our money rules can be very different from other countries. Therefore, people often don't know what they should know. For example, a lady shared with me that her family immigrated to North America when she was 8 years old. Her family believes in higher education, and because she wanted to help many people through her career, her family suggested to her to become a medical doctor. She was the youngest, and she had straight A's all through school, but because her parents had already paid for university for her brother, it wasn't possible for them to pay for her to go to school as well, so she had to work and study at the same time. Little did she know that with her good grades, she could've applied for a scholarship.

You may know similar stories, or not understand the school system at all. We have, in Canada, what we call a RESP, or Registered Education Saving Plan, which we can start when the baby is first born or anytime before the child turns 16. It is not of big use to wait till the child is a teenager, because we want more years of growth for the Education Fund, and it's better to start the plan as soon as possible in order to have more time to add to the return on our investments.

A parent is entitled to receive a Child Tax Benefit in Canada, and the money can be invested in an RESP for the child's further education. Think about it. If your child wants to study to become a medical doctor, a lawyer, or an engineer, it will cost a lot of money, and if you have two or three kids, there is a sum amount of money needed over a very short time, as much as a whole mortgage would be. Could you possibly come up with a few hundred thousand dollars, out of your own pocket, over a number of, let's say, 5 years? That's where an RESP can help to fund for further education. There are also other options through life insurance that you could consider to fund your children's further education. It's important that you understand your options to make the most out of your money.

Protection

The next thing on our budget form asks about the money that is going for protection.

I have mentioned the importance of giving, and the importance of paying yourself first, and now this bill, which goes toward protection (i.e. insurance is equally important. Understanding is needed in order to commit to a bill payment where we may never receive anything from it other than peace of mind, but at the same time, it could well mean that we could continue our lifestyle if we found ourselves in a condition where we couldn't work for a long time, because we had an accident or a critical illness—or in the worst case scenario, we died.

Insurance is not meant to help us get wealthy from the claim. But many families are building wealth using insurance. How? Let me just mention 1 single example to show you:

Let's say you have a family, and you are the bread winner, the person bringing in the money.

You have savings for 3-6 months of living expenses.

You have investments for retirement, and maybe even a business, or money saved up to open a business.

If you have any debts to pay, and you have insurance to protect your income, you can simply build wealth by having an insurance take care of the bills if something happens to you, and you can protect your savings from being used up while you can't work. You won't put more money into your bank account by claiming insurance, but you won't have to pull out your investments and savings, or even go into debt because you now aren't able to earn an income.

Now you will understand the importance of paying a bill that seems to only take money out of your bank account and not have any benefit to it.

We protect our families from going into debt or losing their lifestyle.

Emergency Fund

If you are already putting money away for an emergency fund, or you have 3-6 months savings for that matter, you can have peace of mind and move on, but most people I meet up with have very little savings, if any at all, for if something should happen.

I was talking the other day with a lady who I have known for many years, and when I resigned from my health care career, she told me she was looking into going into business for herself and eventually being able to let go of her job, as she found that it wore her out physically over the years. I suggested I could help her on the financial side of planning to open her own business, but at that time, she doubted herself and said she just couldn't see herself taking on the risk of going into debt to invest in a business.

A year later, she still had the dream, but I realized it had shrunk, and she figured that she would just have to take on some extra hours to save more money if she ever wanted to leave her job. This lady now, after 4 years, has no savings, and she is afraid that if the slightest thing breaks down, she will have to go into debt on top of what she owes, and she is very stressed out because of her financial situation.

I want to tell you that having an emergency fund is not a wish, and it's not something we should consider one day. It's something to get on today, not tomorrow—and don't tell me that you can't save some money, if you have a job. It's a decision you have to make. It's not an option. If you don't have any money to set aside, here are a few ideas: Take on some extra hours at your job, and put that money away. If you think that you will just have to pay more taxes if you do so, you need to sit down with me and have a discussion about that, because I can show you a number of ways to reduce your taxes—yes, legally reduce your taxes, and put more money into your pocket or keep more money in your pocket.

Another way to add to your emergency fund is to sell any item you haven't used in the last 6 months. You can have a garage sale, sell them on eBay, or use whatever other ways there are of selling stuff on the internet, and put that money into an emergency fund. If you are dining out, stop dining out until you have your emergency fund funded. It is more important to have an emergency fund than dining out or having many purses or items in your closet or household, which you can get away with not having.

Another way of looking into where to find money is to sit down with a financial professional and look over all your income and expenses; and together, you will most likely find money going somewhere that you didn't know you could save. I am not kidding. I find money for my clients all the time, and you should not be surprised that it could happen to you. Try it.

Once you have that emergency fund established, you will see good things happen to you. First, it gives you peace of mind. Then it gives you confidence. You can walk taller, face situations at work with a calm approach, and look people in the eye if they want to challenge you. You can make decisions now that won't affect your family negatively, and you can buy into a good deal if the opportunity presents itself.

We all know that sooner or later we will have to replace our car for a newer one, or that over time we will have to buy new appliances, and when the need is there, we have the money available to do so. On your budget form that you will find on my website to print, you have a spot to fill in whether you have an emergency fund fully saved, started, or not started. If you have started it, keep adding to it, and if you haven't, well, commit to start putting money into a savings plan, and don't stop until you have at least 6 months of expenses covered.

Debt Services

Another part of the budget form is designed to write down your amounts of debt services. There are multiple ways of paying off debt faster. It takes discipline to do so, but you can do it. The same way as starting or even forcing yourself to have that emergency fund, you need to tackle the debt service.

If you are using the debt roll-up option, and you are very disciplined doing so, you will have it working for you. If you need a little jumpstart for it, go and make a few hundred dollars extra, and put that towards your smallest amount of debt, and keep going that way until the debt is gone.

We need to work on our bad debt until we don't have it anymore. Sometimes it means consolidating our debt, if it's possible, and sometimes it means that we are not buying things we want and don't need until that debt is paid off. Remember, we often tend to buy things with money we don't have, to impress people who don't care. Stop caring what people think about you. It's none of your business what they think, and they don't offer to pay your bills, after all. Why should you care?

It's your responsibility to be responsible with money, and it's totally okay if you can't have everything to look sharp, cool, or rich while you are striving to make ends meet. It is time that we North Americans smarten up and change our way of thinking. I am not talking about living below your means; I am talking about being responsible so that you can have a lifestyle with peace of mind, knowing you are a good steward with your money.

We see more people at an older age carrying higher debt than ever before. I find at least two reasons for that: One is a lack of understanding of how money works, and the other is that we have a lot of immigrants coming to our country to have a better lifestyle, and they start off late to build wealth. Many come to our country and have to support family back in their home country, and they aren't able to save money for themselves for a very long time. And many are re-mortgaging their house many times during their life to have access to extra money. The sad part is when the money goes to something that doesn't build wealth. We need to lead by example and get out of bad debt. We can do it, even though the task is not easy.

"I've never been poor,
only broke.
Being poor is a frame of mind.
Being broke is only a
temporary decision."
– Mike Todd

Investments

Investments is an area that has many shades: bright ones, dark ones, and many in between. We have people coming into our country from all walks of life, and people who are born and raised here. The message that almost all of them have is to buy real estate to build wealth and have a great retirement.

The same thing that I would say when it comes to any investment, I would say about real estate: If you don't understand real estate, don't invest in real estate.

I understand that people are hesitant about the stock market after seeing so many people losing their money in 2008 and 2011, but that doesn't mean that the stock market isn't working to build wealth.

When we understand investments, we can see that there are great ways to get a good rate of return. When we use the investment strategies that the wealthy people use, there is definitely a good return on our investment.

I find that if people would start putting the same amount of time into learning how money works as they put into listening to news, they would all be well educated on money matters—and guess what? Not listening to the news is also beneficial because we wouldn't hear all that bad chatter about the market going down, and then get emotionally affected by it. We always make money in the market when we understand dollar-cost averaging, investing for the long term, not pulling our money out when the market is down, etc. I encourage everyone to learn more about investments and stop listening to people who don't know much about investments, or to people who suggest that only real estate is good. You can invest in real estate without owning a property, and you can buy physical real estate. Just know what the difference is and how it works. The same goes for all other investments.

The reason why I mention real estate more than other investments is not that I am against investing in real estate. I am investing in real estate myself, and I believe it's a good way of investing. Are you buying a house for your family, or are you buying rental properties? Both have their good and bad sides. If you buy to live in your house instead of renting, do the math on what it will cost you to maintain it, plus the interest you will pay on a mortgage, and the property taxes. If you realize a gain, by all means, buy your house. It's something that can eventually appreciate in value, and as your own family resident, you don't pay capital gains tax on it; but if you buy your house with the intention of selling it one day in your retirement to live of the money, just consider that you still need to live somewhere when you retire, and your retirement won't be cheap, after all. We need other money besides the money sitting in our house.

If you buy to rent, do the math. If, after all the expenses, taxes, and labour that goes into it, you are left with a positive cash flow, and extra money for repairs and vacancies, you may be okay. Look into what accounts of investments you have for the long term. I had a lady coming into my office one day, telling me that she was paying so much tax on the money she had to withdraw from her RRSP account that she was afraid she would run out of money in a few years, and she also mentioned that she had never paid attention to where her investment banker had invested her money. All she knew was that her banker had mentioned that her investment was doing great, and she left it up to her husband to make the decisions where to put the money. I invited her to my workshop on how money works, and after a bit of hesitation because of her age, and not having a long investment horizon ahead of her, she decided to come and learn more. After the first class, she asked me, "Why wouldn't my banker have ever mentioned any other types of accounts than RRSPs? Well, maybe he did but just very casually. Or maybe not, because of not knowing or under-standing other options. I don't know the answer, but had this lady had proper understanding on how money works, she could have made smarter decisions on where to invest her money so that she wouldn't have to pay that much tax in her retirement, or any taxes at all. Now she had lost her husband and was all by herself, having to go back to work for maybe as long as she lives, to have the money needed to live. Her husband had always told her that she would be okay when he was gone, because they both had a pension and a lot of savings. He also had trusted the banker, not understanding the game of money. If it's all you do, get understanding before you trust anyone with your money.

"If you were born poor, it's not your mistake,
but if you die poor, it's your mistake."
– Warren Buffet

Bonus Budgeting Forms at www.YourOwnPayToday.com

∞ Questions for Success ∞

* What is the most helpful idea from this chapter for you?

*When was the last time you did a financial overview?

* On a scale from 1-10, where would you rate yourself on knowing the money game?

*Do you have a monthly budget you live by, or are you financially able to live a lifestyle where you don't have to be concerned about money?

* Below, write down what you need to take care of that has been mentioned in this chapter:

1._____

_____

2._____

_____

3._____

_____

4._____

_____

∞ Chapter Nine ∞

Don't Leave Any Money on the Table, Step 8

Work While You Can, When You Can

Some of my clients have told me that they don't want to work extra time at their job or any other work because they will pay more taxes at the end of the day and won't keep more money in their pocket.

"Work while you can, when you can" does not precisely mean that you should have two or three different jobs, because—look at this—if you work for money, you will be paying taxes on earned money.

If you make more money, you will be in a higher tax bracket; and yes, therefore, you could end up paying more taxes.

It is not just about making more money but about generating more income, and structuring it in a way that works for you.

There are a number of ways you can make more money, and you should make as much money as you can.

If you can put that extra money into your savings, or pay off your debt sooner, why wouldn't you?

When I came to Canada, in 2009, and started working after I got certified as a health care aid, I found that with only one income, I wouldn't be able to pay all my bills.

It is rather sad that we live in one of the wealthiest countries in the world but have so little knowledge about money and the money rules that we should know but we don't.

I was fortunate to have entrepreneurial blood, and started looking for ways to improve my financial situation. I had not come to Canada to be broke. I knew, if I wanted to have a better shot in life, I had to do something about it, and search for ways to learn more and do better.

Five years after arriving in Canada, I was ready to start my own business. For me, it meant to learn the game of money and play it right. For you, it may be something different, and that's okay. What I wish for you is that you have learned some things that you can apply in your financial plan that will help you do better, and I encourage you to go a step or 2 further into learning how money works, because you are working with money every single day, and knowing more will definitely help you keep more money in your own pocket.

If you have a business, you are already way ahead of those who are working for an employer, but it's possible that you don't know all the advantages to keep more money or to structure it with a holistic financial plan.

If you are only working for a boss, I recommend that you look for some extra income on a part time basis—not taking extra shifts and coming home more tired, more broke, or even more frustrated. I know that today we have more money making opportunities than we ever had before. It doesn't matter in what part of the world you live.

If nothing else, get into a multi-level marketing company that has a great training system, and learn to be an entrepreneur, have the mindset of an entrepreneur, and learn great social skills. That also can put some extra money into your pocket. Then learn more about taxes and how money works overall, and you will have a big jump start in your financial situation. A disclaimer though: There is no free lunch—what you put in, you will get out. Don't expect to get involved in a marketing company and not have to pay anything. And don't expect that everything will fall from the sky for your benefit. No, not at all—you sign up, you show up, and you learn and follow the system, and the system will support you. If you put in more effort, you will receive more benefits; if you put in less, you will get less. It's an opportunity, not a lottery.

Pay in Cash

Those were the days, you may say; and many don't carry cash at all anymore.

Let's take a look at some benefits of carrying cash:

When we pull the money out of our wallet to pay, we can physically feel that we are giving something of value to another person, and it registers differently in our brain than when we swipe a card and not see any numbers.

When we use credit to pay, we need to track the amount and the receipt, and it has very little impact on our emotions; but in our minds, we carry the thought that we need to pay, and what it does psychologically is to work in the opposite way from when we receive pay, and we are operating on a different frequency.

When we pay in cash, we also can use the envelope system.

How to use the envelope system:

On your budget form, you can see the exact amount of money needed for groceries, toiletries, clothing, laundry detergent, vacation, entertainment, medical, hair care, bills, etc. You can withdraw the amount needed from your checking account, and divide it into different envelopes named for each category, and discipline yourself to only use the amount of money that you put in for that specific group or item. This gives you more discipline over your money, and if something comes up that you hadn't planned for, it would be easier to say no, because there would not be any monies left. You may have some months where you use less than you had planned for, and that can be thrown into your emergency fund now, or transferred over to the next month in case you suddenly should need some extra in that category.

Look for Great Deals

When you have the habit of making a shopping list, you can look for coupons to save, or you can buy some items when they are on sale while you are out shopping, if you know you will need them that month. Sometimes certain stores carry lower prices as well, and you could go there to get your groceries. I would not suggest driving through town for 1-2 lower priced items if you can buy it close by for just a little bit more, because it not only takes your time but also costs you going across town, and may not save you anything.

Wait to buy clothes when they are on sale, or buy online if that saves you money.

How often are you asking for a better deal?

It all comes down to financial knowledge. If you know the steps to take beforehand, you can think it through and make better decisions.

I could ask someone, who bought a vehicle and went through the whole process, to tell me about it, and I would then know what process I would go through when buying a car, if it is my first time and I have no knowledge about the process. It may be a different model I am buying, or a different dealer I go to, but the knowledge that someone can share with me may help me to ask the questions I should ask, or to know what I should be aware of.

It is the same thing when someone has gone through the experience of planning for a funeral of a loved one. Don't you think we could learn from their experience? Absolutely! It doesn't mean that those people should be our financial go-to people. They may be well experienced in one area, but they only can share about that one experience they had. Still, we can learn from each other.

Don't rush into buying. Although it is said that successful people make decisions really quickly, and hardly ever change them, this is not what that means.

If you are looking for a thing to buy, and the sales person tells you that the deal will only last till the end of the day, and that you will never find that deal again, but you don't have the money to buy, and you would have to go into debt doing so, then re-think it. It may be that the deal would be gone, but it also may be that you would have *buyers regret*, because you were rushed to buy. In any case, use common sense, and rely on your 6th sense that will guide you to make the decision to buy or to wait.

Set up Automatic Payments

Life can pass by very quickly, and we all can be so busy that before we know it, a month is up and a bill is due to be paid. Have you ever had that happen to you, where you forgot about a bill, and you just completely missed it? And you even got charged an extra fee because you paid late? It has happened to me, and I don't like the extra fee. It's also not fair to the person or company that provides the service to me. They have bills to pay too.

Part of our financial planning should be setting up automatic payments. It saves me time, I don't have it on my schedule and my mind, but it's taken care of. It saves me from getting extra charges, and my service provider gets the money on time.

With today's technology, we have all the tools we need to set it up and track it. Tracking is important if you have automatic payments or are sending a check.

I had a very bad experience with my phone company in Manitoba, with automatic payments. Month after month, I had to call them and ask why they took my payment twice. Every time, I would get the same response, "Oh, we are so sorry; we have new staff, and they made a mistake. We will reverse the payment." Then, I had to check my account to see if they actually did reverse the payment. If that had only happened one single time, I would not even mention it. It not only happened to me, but it happened to many other people in the area too. It happened many times with the same company, and it was always the new staff that made the mistake! Really? How much staff turnover can a company have before they just acknowledge that they need to fix the problem once and for all? That is very upsetting, and it should never be that way, but for that same reason, even if automatic payments can save you time and money, we still need to track and keep a balanced spreadsheet.

Some people don't have the need to look at a budget before they buy something, because they have a lot of money, but that's not how they started. They are at the income level now that they can afford to spend for pleasure as they like, but until you are at that level, you will do better by telling your money where to go, by living on a budget. It may be a very luxurious budget, and good for you. It may also be good to start to track where your money is going, and that is the point. Tell your money where to go instead of seeing your money run away.

Have a Business

Write your own paycheck! That is the title of this book. You can only make a certain amount of money by trading your time for money. If you have specialized knowledge in your field, you may be paid very well for your service and have very good money coming into your bank account, but if you are working for someone to get paid that well, or for just an average wage or salary, it's not how much money you make that counts; it's how much you keep.

Robert Kiyosaki explains it so well in his book, *Rich Dad, Poor Dad*, when he talks about the "cashflow quadrant," and how as an employee, you trade time for money. When you are self-employed, you own a job. When you are a business owner, you have people working for you. When you are an investor, you have money working for you.

In my opinion, everyone should have a side hustle or a business. It gives you the drive to get up in the morning and the energy at night. It expands your vision, and it makes you stronger. It allows you to receive tax advantages, and it gives you flexibility. It allows you to earn more with less effort, and you can provide income to many by creating a job for them.

Running a business is a lot of work, and it may sound like I am contradicting myself. Any startup of a business requires long days of work, and many times, it won't pay you right away. You have to have a vision to see that the results will come sooner or later, and *keep on keeping on* until that happens.

That's why it makes you stronger. That's why you put in the effort. You use your brain, whereas working for someone else doesn't exactly make you think. Even if you think you are thinking, you may not be. Your brain runs most of the time on auto pilot, or you think about things that happened in the past, which is not thinking at all—it's only mental activity and remembering things. Thinking happens when we come up with ideas that we can use to do things in a better way or a different way. Thinking happens when we imagine things, and when we get creative.

Having a business is a mindset. If you think you can run a business, you can. If you think you can't, you are right; you can't. Why not give it a try?

In North America, we are highly encouraged by our government to have a business. A business man or woman receives tax advantages and, therefore, can invest more money back into the business.

When I worked as an employee, I soon realized that the harder I worked, the more money I earned, the more taxes I had to pay. Many of my clients say that too. Some of them only work the bare minimum that they have to, in order to not get into a higher tax bracket. That is also from a lack of financial education, and sometimes from being ignorant. It's not enough to earn the minimum and think we can fund our retirement with that. It's not how much money we make that will give us the return or results we are looking for; it's the understanding, strategizing, and applying knowledge that will take us there.

In the times we live in today, we have more opportunities than ever before to make some money as a self-employed person. Technology has enabled us to buy and sell all over the world, and we are not bound to only one location. With a little bit of thinking, we can come up with many great ideas to have a side hustle. Ideas are useless though until we act upon them.

I encourage you to write your own paycheck. If you, at one point, had a dream that you wanted to see come true, and over time you gave up on that dream, it's time to re-ignite that dream again, and take action to pursue it. You can do it. You have all it takes.

Have a Financial Mentor

When you look for a financial mentor, look for someone who has the heart of a teacher and is an expert in the field.

They should be someone who explains everything in a very simple way so that you can understand, and they should be more concerned with teaching you instead of making the sale.

They are someone who empowers you through education to make the best decision with your money.

If you need help to find a trusted financial expert that I can endorse in your area, go to www.YourOwnPayToday.com.

∞ Questions for Success ∞

* What was the most helpful idea from this chapter for you?

* What are 3 benefits of using cash instead of credit?

* Do you have a financial mentor?

* Do you have a side hustle or a business?

* Write down 4 success steps you will take to apply your knowledge:

1._____

_____

2._____

_____

3._____

_____

4._____

_____

∞ Chapter 10 ∞

Responsibilities and Commitment

Last Will and Testament

A will is a legal document that serves to leave your wishes behind for your family to follow, and to distribute your property to those of your choosing. You can assign specific people to receive items from your estate, and you can indicate how you want your property divided. If you have appointed an executor, he or she will carry out those wishes.

A will also allows you to assign someone to take care of your underage children, as a legal guardian who will be responsible for their wellbeing when you are no longer there, until they reach the age of adulthood.

It is vitally important to have your wishes documented. Your estate would have to go through probate, and all your assets that are taxable would go through a screening process that needs an accountant, a lawyer, and an executor. The accountant's job is to figure out what the taxable amount is on your estate. The lawyer does all the legal stuff, and when all taxes are paid, the process to divide the estate now can take place, and the heirs receive what is left after taxes, the accountant's fee, legal fees, and all outstanding fees have been paid.

If there are minors involved, a will gives the executor guidance on what to do and how to act on their behalf. Your wishes will be followed, and your family will be taken care of in the way you had planned it. When you have a will, you have peace of mind.

What happens if you don't have a will? The government has a standard will that will be used to take care of your estate, and if you have underage children, the government will decide where they will go. It may well be that you wouldn't want that to happen, because they don't know your kids, your relatives, or anything related to your family, and they will go by what they find is the best for them so that they will receive shelter, clothing, and schooling—but what about family? Feeling accepted? Belonging? What if the siblings get separated and go to different homes?

It's your responsibility to take care of this, and it does not take more than a little bit of your time and planning. You can make a will with an attorney, or you can do it yourself. If you have questions on how to do it, you should seek out professional help, but don't leave this important task for another day. It's part of your financial planning.

Power of Attorney for Health

A power of attorney for health is also called a *living will*. It's a legal document that serves to make decisions about your health while you are still alive but can't communicate because of health issues (for example, if a person has a stroke and loses the ability to speak). It may be temporary, but medical decisions have to be made, and someone needs to make those decisions. It can be extremely difficult for the family when

they don't know what to do. If you already have it documented, it can be followed according to your personal wishes
for that specific situation, and your family doesn't have to
make those difficult choices.

When should you get your living will done? My answer is:
today. It is one thing I always include in my financial planning
with my clients.

Some years ago, one of my lady friends, in her early 50s,
had a severe stroke. She was a healthy person, and we were
all surprised that it happened to her. One day, she was just not
feeling well but didn't think it was anything to worry about.
But as the day went on, she got really consumed by it. She
called her brother while she was about to leave the house to
go and check on her aging mother in the care home. While on
the phone with her brother, she collapsed and had a severe
stroke. She lost the ability of speech, and her brother had to
step into her shoes now to make decisions on her behalf—but
not his decisions, because she had her living will in place, and
her brother could now carry out what she had preplanned.

Can you see yourself in a situation where you have to
decide on someone else's life decisions? What if your mother
or father were the one having to go through difficult health
challenges, and no document was there to guide you? And you
now had to make the final decisions of what you think would
be in the best interest of your parent—and then there is that
sibling of yours that has a completely different view on the
situation; so then what?

I could go on and on with many examples of how important
a living will is, but I think you get my point.

We are never too young to write down our wishes. We see so many young people needing care because of an accident they had, or because of cancer or even MS, which is affecting so many fairly young people.

You can go to an attorney to make a living will, or you can do it yourself with a package that you can download or purchase, which will be standard, where you only have to fill in the blanks, but it may be of importance to you to have a customized document. There are different ways that you can do it, but the main thing is: Do it!

Power of Attorney for Property

A power of attorney is a legal document that gives someone else the right to act on your behalf, for your property, bank accounts, investments, business, etc.

It is just as important to have this document as it is to have your last will and testament and your living will.

You never know what could happen or when, where you are still alive but have no way of taking care of your personal property, and you need someone who can step in for you until you are able to do it yourself again.

Here again, we often think that these are things we can take care of later in life to prepare for our old age, but because we never know if we will be able to do it when we push it away for later, it's better to have it and not use it than to not have it and run into a lot of problems.

In my previous career, I have observed aging parents. We see them going out for dinner or to a doctor's appointment, and everything seems to be okay, but often, when we take a closer look, we can notice some forgetfulness or confusion, and even if it's a minor thing, dramatic financial mistakes can occur, and someone needs to step in, but with what right? None, if there is no power of attorney. At this point, it may be too late to make one, because the person has to be of sound mental health while doing so. After all, this is a vital important decision to sign off on everything, and the person should be of sound health in order to do so and to make wise decisions. Therefore, we should do it sooner than later.

I don't want to go into legal advice here; you should seek out a professional to create these documents. However, you most likely have heard about frozen bank accounts and such, which all can be avoided by proper planning and creating the supporting documents.

Why do we push these things off for later? Read on to find out...

Peace of Mind

When my boys became teenagers, we wanted to create more space for them to hang out with their peers at home, and we planned a major house renovation, which was due anyway. First, we thought it would be the one room, plus a few others with minor stuff, but altogether, it would take quite a bit of work. When we started the process, we found there was way more to it than we had thought before we started, and a 2-3 week project became a 2-month project. Sometimes we would say that had we known, we may not even have started.

When it comes to planning our financial house, it's almost like renovating a house, isn't it? We seek out professional help because we need an insurance policy, but when we take a look at our holistic plan, we realize that our pension plan is still with our former employer and needs to be transferred into a LIRA, or we don't have a will or power of attorneys for health and property, or we could pay our house off in less time if we took a different approach, and so on and so on. It can suddenly seem like a lot, and we may think of just not doing it at all because it seems overwhelming, and we may leave it for the next time, but it is not less work later than it is right now. We better just get on to it and get it done. It's a matter of time to plan, and even if it takes a week, how much difference does a week's time really make in our daily life? Not much. The peace of mind it gives you once it's all done is worth it.

Some years ago, I had purchased an estate planning package through one of the product providers I work with. It gave me the amount of insurance needed to cover funeral expenses, had all the customized legal documents, and offered a concierge service at the time of death. I had created my own will, living will, and power of attorney back then, but we go through changes all our lives, don't we? I had a little grandson since, and I had moved to a different province to expand my business, and I do travel a fair amount because of my business, so I knew I needed to update my legal documents, but it always didn't seem to fit into my schedule. Does that sound familiar to you?

Just so that you know, I am a human being just like you, and although I have all it takes to just go and get it done, it doesn't happen by accident. I had to schedule in some time to get on to it and do it. I remember that it was a Sunday afternoon, and I figured I could get to it and make the needed changes, and while I was working on it, a friend of mine contacted me and asked if I had some time to go for coffee. My response was that I was in the middle of getting my legal documents up to date, and it almost freaked out my friend. She asked me, "Is everything okay with you?" Absolutely, but I needed it done so I could have peace of mind. I encouraged my friend to get hers taken care of too. How about you? Are you like my friend who thought it was something we only do when we think we are close to our departure from this world? I hope you have seen the importance of doing it while you are capable and healthy. It does give you tremendous peace of mind.

Time with Family

Last week I attended a financial workshop, and the instructor asked all of us to write down 3 things we would do if we had all the money we needed and we had plenty of time on hand.

People had different answers, but most of them said they would spend more time with their family. What about you? What would you have answered?

We can be so busy with our jobs, with running errands, birthday parties, weddings, church activities, school events, sports, etc. One day starts and goes by so swiftly, and the next one is just as busy; and before long, a week has gone by, and then a month, and then it is the end of the year again. Right?

What does time with the family have to do with writing your own paycheck, or with becoming financially independent?

Life is short and precious, and we have already stated that we would like to have more time with family, but living a life in a vicious rat race will hardly allow us the desired time for family.

My dad would always say that he wanted all of us kids to be self-employed so that we could control our time, and not depend on having to clock in at a certain time and be tied up for a number of hours. He knew the difference between being an employee and being self-employed, and he did not want us to experience the employee side.

I have been self-employed for the majority of my life, but I am grateful for the experience I had as an employee for a couple of years. I can relate to my fellow colleagues, who are still working for a paycheck while building up their team and becoming self-employed, and to my clients who depend on a job.

As a business owner, we work more hours, go on less vacations, and stay up later or get up earlier than most employees do, but we are not bound to a certain location for a number of hours on any given day. We can take the time to volunteer or help a family member, or visit someone in the hospital, or babysit unexpectedly, or so many other things— because we can shift our workload around, or we can leverage other people to do the work for us. This also gives us more flexibility to spend time with family.

Often, I think everyone should have a side hustle, where they can involve the family so that they can spend more time together, and also have multiple sources of income to leave as a legacy for the family. It definitely stretches our vision; we become more creative, and most likely are more positive as well. Think about it.

A few years ago, I decided to build a garden shed in my backyard, and because I love to get my hands on different things and experience all sorts of work, I asked my oldest son, who was living with me at that time, if he would be interested in making it a summer project together—to build the shed from scratch—and he was. We took some measurements, ordered the material for the shed, and got to work. I had learned some carpentry from my dad when I was a teenager, and I could pass on that knowledge to my son. We had an amazing time together while putting the shed together piece by piece, and finally, after two weeks of working on it, the shed was finished—painted and done. I could've gone and bought a garden shed and had it placed in my backyard, but we would have missed out on the joy of having spent that time together.

What are things you would like to do with your family? We can do so many things other than sitting in front of the TV set. We may be together while watching TV, but will we remember? I am sure my son will remember the time we spent together while building the shed, but he would forget what movie we had watched, sitting in the living room. Build memories that last for a long time. Doing something that contributes to life with our loved ones will always be treasured.

Love and Listen More

Dr. Napoleon Hill took on the task of interviewing thousands and thousands of people. Andrew Carnegie challenged him with the task because he had gained such a fortune in the first half of his life that he was considered to be one of the wealthiest people in America. Carnegie devoted the first half of his life to gaining riches, and the second half to giving it all away. He did not intend to give it to people on the street; he wanted his riches to continue to make an impact in this world. Therefore, he wanted to know what qualities the people he would give it to should possess, so that the wealth he had built up would continue to do good in this world long after he was gone.

This was not an easy task, and that is why he challenged Dr. Hill, a reporter, to interview thousands of people to find out what the habits and the reasons were behind people's wealth, and what differentiates the wealthy from the average person. Based on the findings, over a period of 20 years, he could disburse his wealth to the right people. Hill found that wealthy people are people who think for themselves. They listen more and talk less. Another very important factor that Dr. Hill found was that most people came to their senses only after they reached the age of forty, and that most wealth was created by people between the ages of forty and sixty, or even later.

Don't we find that grandparents listen more to their grandkids than they did to their kids, and they share more love to the grandkids than they did to their own kids? That may not be the case, but it could well be that way because they are over forty.

I am over forty, and I know for a fact that I am much more patient now than I was when I was younger. I listen more, and I have much more understanding for people when things don't go the way they expected. There is definitely something about a mature age, but we don't have to wait until we get older to show more affection and more love to people, and to listen more.

Often, we hear the expression, "If I could live life all over again, I would do things differently." Maybe. But we have today, and that is what counts. What was yesterday is pretty much irrelevant, and we can learn from it but not change it; so let's do our best with what we have today, and our tomorrow can be better.

Travel More

I remember the few times when my parents took us to a hot water spring to spend a day, and the field trips we made, and when we wandered through the mountains to check up on the cattle. Those are times that will always stay with me, and those were also times when we took distance from our daily activities, out of our comfort zone, and we were open to new things—we saw different things than we did at home or on the farm.

We need to take some distance and go out of our comfort zone in order to expand our vision. People who never travel are like a storybook with only one single page.

It is not so much the amount of time but the quality of time we can have with each other. I live a pretty busy life, with my team and clients in different provinces across Canada, and I travel a lot for work and very little for vacation; but I have been so fortunate to be able to spend time with my kids in Hawaii, Cancun a number of times, New Orleans, San Francisco, and many other locations, and it is rewarding to be able to do that.

So many people never travel, be it for lack of money or that they don't get time off work, or because they need to spend the time at home when they are off work.

135

I go on a company trip once a year—not for business but for expanding my vision, and to learn new lifestyles, taste different food, and experience different cultures, weather, and languages. Life is too short to just stay in one place all our lives. If we plan to travel, we would be able to, but we have to plan it. It's the same as with everything else: We don't plan to fail; we just fail to plan.

Volunteer More

Everyone needs help sometime in life, and it's a great and rewarding feeling to be able to help someone.

Volunteering is a lifestyle. It helps the student to get more knowledge for their work experience, and it opens our minds for things we don't see otherwise.

∞ Questions for Success ∞

* What is the most helpful idea from this chapter for you?

* Have you taken this step and made your last will and testament, power of attorney, and living will?

* What are things you could do with your loved ones to spend more time together?

* Which places would you want to travel to?

* Below, write 3 things you would do if you had all the money you needed and all the time to spend it:

1._____

_____

Write Your Own Paycheck

2._____

_____

3._____

_____

4._____

_____

About the Author

Katharina grew up on a dairy and grain farm in a very small community in Mexico.

Fate took her through various lessons of life, through deep valleys and over mountain tops, which prepared her to face bigger challenges and go into deeper waters.

She has been very involved in the field of music since 1984.

She managed a distribution centre of natural pathology products for a number of years, where she first learned about the miraculous healing power through nature.

In 2006, she got introduced to her first life coach, and emerged herself in studying the laws of the Universe with the great teachers from the movie, *The Secret*.

She immigrated to Canada in 2009, and revamped herself, going back to school and becoming a certified health care attendant with the intention of finishing her nursing career. But life happened to her again, and through a nasty accident, she found herself needing to leave her career and rethink life.

She went back to college one more time and wrote her exams for financial services, and has been an independent financial representative since 2015. Dedicated to financial literacy, she believes you can change your life by changing the way you think.

Katharina travels all across Canada to service her clients, and currently works out of her office in North York, Toronto.